LADY OF THE CHASE

The life and hunting diaries of Daphne Moore

To Tessa

Without whose support and encouragement this book,
and much else, would not have been possible.

LADY OF THE CHASE

The life and hunting diaries
of Daphne Moore

Alastair Jackson

MERLIN UNWIN BOOKS

First published in Great Britain by Merlin Unwin Books Ltd, 2018

Merlin Unwin Books Ltd
Palmers House
7 Corve Street
Ludlow
Shropshire SY8 1DB
U.K.

www.merlinunwin.co.uk

ISBN 978-1-910723-76-0

Typeset in 12 point Bembo by Merlin Unwin Books

Printed by Leo Paper Products

Contents

Hunt Staff Benefit Society (HSBS)

The Hunt Staff Benefit Society is a pension scheme available to all those working as employees of Hunts, whether as huntsmen, whippers-in, kennelmen, countrymen, or Hunt grooms. It is highly subsidised, with all administration and regulatory expenses currently covered by fundraising and by subscriptions and donations from supporters of hunting. The Society is particularly lucky to have the Prince of Wales as its Patron and Governor.

There is also a charity run in tandem with the HSBS, known as the Hunt Servants' Fund, which is able to help Hunt staff, their widows and dependants, in all sorts of ways if they find themselves in difficulties.

Right: Brass buttons showing the HSBS logo.

The owner of Daphne Moore's hunting diaries, Michael O'Reilly, is donating all his royalties to the Hunt Staff Benefit Society.

Foreword

BY SIMON HART MP

For several years Daphne Moore's comprehensive hunting diaries adorned my book shelves but provided only me with the pleasure of reading them.

The first one I picked up (after they arrived in a plastic bag following her death) recounted the last full season before the outbreak of war in 1939. I was hooked by the poignancy of her writing and the way in which she so beautifully described what clearly felt to her like the end of everything in the world worth caring about. It was to preserve this way of life that she had become a founder member of the BFSS in 1930, contributing a five shilling subscription and remaining a member until her death.

I doubt very much she thought these accounts would get the wider scrutiny that this book provides. They were personal accounts leaving no detail unrecorded. Each entry was a transcript of the day's proceedings. Who was there, what they wore, who they were with and what they talked about. She reserved a very special space for the hounds about whom she spoke not as modern writers do about animals, with a synthetically exaggerated affection, but with a practical sense of devotion and respect.

She records my father's first day with the Cotswold Vale (they became great friends) when my Uncle Chris whipped as Tony Wright's father Sam was on holiday. The idea that a whipper-in should take any holiday once hunting had started was an anathema to Daphne and soon became one for my father too!

Her accounts of the heyday of otter hunting, particularly with Ronnie Wallace when he was hunting the Hawkstone is more of a chapter in the social history of the UK than it is an analysis of this long-gone form of hunting.

So it's thanks to Michael O'Reilly that this period in the long history of hunting gets the airing it deserves. Daphne's immaculate, detailed and comprehensive account of over 50 glorious years has been delightfully revived by Alastair Jackson and it should be a compulsory read for everyone involved in hunting as it so cleverly puts into words why we do it, and why we fight for it, and why it has survived.

Alastair Jackson, Joint Master and Huntsman of the Cattistock, at the opening meet in 1988.

Acknowledgements

I was aware of the existence of Daphne Moore's hunting diaries as, on her death in 2004, they had been delivered to my office when I was Director of the Masters of Foxhounds Association. They were to be passed on to Simon Hart, a former Master of Foxhounds and now an MP and Chairman of the Countryside Alliance, who had inherited them from Daphne. I remember at the time being entranced by this collection of diaries, which she had kept from 1930, when she was 20 years old, liberally illustrated with her own miniature drawings and many photographs.

It was then with complete surprise that I received a telephone call in the winter of 2016 from Michael O'Reilly, a keen enthusiast of hunting and its history, who had acquired the diaries from Simon Hart, asking me if I would consider writing a book on the life of Daphne Moore, based on these diaries. Not only was he keen on the concept of a book, but he wished to give all the royalties to the Hunt Staff Benefit Society, and so, naturally, I was delighted to accept.

My initial research into the Moore family history was helped enormously by the fame of her brother, the well-known author and naturalist, John Moore. Valerie Haworth, secretary of the John Moore Society and editor of their journal, has been of enormous help, as

has the chairman, Alan Freeman. Curator of the John Moore Museum, Simon Lawton, gave valuable advice, as did local historian, John Dixon. Beryl Warren, who used to farm at Bredon, is one of the few people today who knew Daphne Moore in her early days and provided invaluable personal detail. Tim Holland-Martin, who as a child rode regularly with Daphne, was of enormous help over the years that she worked for his family, as was his cousin, Lady Penelope Bossom, whose efficient archive provided some unique photographs of the family.

Of her Badminton days, I was able to talk to Ian Farquhar, Joint Master of the Duke of Beaufort's; Martin Scott, whose father, Bill Scott, features so largely in the diaries; Lord Mancroft, chairman of the Masters of Foxhounds Association, who was brought up in Badminton village; Edward Knowles, who is now Joint Master of the Tedworth, who worked in the Estate Office; and Allan Garrigan, who worked in the kennels.

Of her latter days, Kay Gardner knew Daphne better than most and was generous in her information, as was Harry Parsons of Sealyham terrier fame, who visited her several times in the last year of her life.

Most of the hunting photographs have been provided by Jim Meads, either taken by himself, or by his father Frank H.

Meads. Their extensive archive is unique and is now with the British Sporting Art Trust. David Wallace took great trouble to provide photographs of his father, Captain Ronnie Wallace, and Steve Eggleton found several pre-war images from his collection. Thanks particularly to the John Moore Society, who provided many of the Moore family photographs which have greatly enhanced this book. Pitor Nitecki kindly provided the photo of Charles's Bridge and Adrian Long TTL Video for the photo of Ian Farquhar (page 183). Ian Ware (www.ianwarephotography) kindly took the photographs at Badminton on pages 203-4.

I must also thank Nessie Chanter who undertook the unenviable task of deciphering my handwriting and preparing the manuscript for the publishers, somehow fitting it in with being a Master of the Heythrop Foxhounds, Clerk of the Course at Stratford Racecourse and having a baby.

The publishers themselves, Karen McCall and Merlin Unwin, have worked tirelessly and with great skill and enthusiasm to turn this project into the attractive book that we now see.

Finally, I must thank my good friend Michael Clayton, former editor of *Horse & Hound* for 24 years and author of over 20 books himself, for his advice and enthusiasm throughout this project and for writing the Preface.   AJ

Alastair Jackson, who first met Daphne Moore in the 1960s.

Preface

BY MICHAEL CLAYTON

Daphne Moore came into my life in the early 1960s when I met her at a Portman Hunt puppy show, held at their kennels, beautifully situated at Bryanston, in the hills west of Blandford Forum.
Tall, willowy, and dressed impeccably in a pale mauve two-piece suit, and a close-fitting white hat, Daphne looked every inch the country gentlewoman that she was. She appeared to come from a privileged family background, although this was far from the truth.

I had read her hunting reports and articles in *Horse and Hound* since boyhood, and held her in some reverence as an authority on the sport I loved.

Somewhat to my surprise she greeted me warmly by name, although I was a comparative newcomer as a part-time sporting writer, and was at the time a BBC news reporter.

Daphne was seated in a prime position in the front row, producing an impressive lorgnette to study the Portman's new entry list with close attention. She chatted affably to the senior members of the Hunt, and was in her element. Her fluting voice, aristocratically accented, could be clearly heard several rows back.

Thereafter I continued to meet her at Peterborough Royal Foxhound Show, and at other puppy shows, notably the 10th Duke of Beaufort's at Badminton, one of the highlights in her year. As far as Daphne was concerned, "Master's" pack was the font of all that was good in hound breeding.

It was only when I became Editor of *Horse and Hound*, from 1973, that I became aware just how much Daphne's treasured lifestyle depended on her skill with the pen.

As Alastair Jackson recounts in this biography, Daphne relied heavily on the comparatively sparse income to be derived as a hunting correspondent, compared with many other specialist areas of journalism.

Daphne was the most devoted of enthusiasts, always buoyed up by the immense pleasure she derived from observing hounds, in the hunting field and on the flags, the surface of a show ring. Her highly sensitive nature could also plunge her to the depths of depression and alarm, although she was remarkably adept at regaining her charm and equilibrium.

Those of us who have shared Daphne's love of venery, to whatever degree, will value this long overdue account of her creative achievements despite severe obstacles and set-backs which required courage and persistence to overcome. As she wrote in a second edition of her autobiography in 1994, she was "never blessed with this world's goods". From childhood she experienced her family's financial and social come-down of an abrupt move from a virtual manor to a semi-detached council house, thereafter caring for her widowed mother for many years until her death.

Both world wars had a cruel impact on Daphne's life, the second conflict robbing her of a man she was likely to marry, and additionally her friend and mentor, George, Earl of Coventry, Master of the Croome hounds she adored following.

None of the poignant aspects of her life appeared in her stoic autobiography. Alastair Jackson has lifted the veil on the full story of her life through access to her private diaries, maintained assiduously in great detail, which was never published in her lifetime.

There is little emotion in these diaries but Alastair's own researches have filled in the full story of her life and its vicissitudes.

Much is owed to the hunting enthusiast Michael O'Reilly who acquired the diaries, appreciated their worth, and has sponsored their publication as the formation of this new biography.

Alastair Jackson has produced a fascinating account of the life of a woman of remarkable qualities and resolve, bearing witness to the life-shattering rigours of the 20th century endured with fortitude and dignity.

For Daphne the Second World War followed an idyllic period of foxhunting, mounted and on foot, and otter hunting in the summer

A very typical photograph of Daphne Moore, seated four from the left, attending the Heythrop Puppy Show in the 1970s. Sitting next to her in the large sun hat is her good friend Miss 'Tuppy' Pearson, who drove her to many events.

months. Those who are prejudiced against otter hunting will learn much about its appeal, and its practice, from Daphne's detailed account of long days on the riversides with hounds. She was horrified by the slaughter of whole packs of hounds soon after war was declared.

Working as a groom, delivering a daily milk round, and heavy farm labour, were all part of her wartime lot, and it says much for her core of determination that she carried out these tasks, despite various injuries and occasional difficulties in working under long-serving staff.

Her many years of running or cycling in pursuit of hounds, made her remarkably fit and contributed to her lifetime of 94 years.

Daphne Moore hunting with the Croome in the mid-1930s on a horse called Sam, one of many passing through the hands of farmer and horse dealer, Harry Gittins. Daphne hunted his horses, many of them very green and completely unknown to her, on a regular basis.

Alastair Jackson has carefully allowed Daphne's own personal diary to shine through the narrative. His own researches, and his deep knowledge of hunting, as a distinguished former Master of Foxhounds, amateur huntsman and hound breeder, enable him to provide an authoritative background.

Daphne's frank assessment of people and events, sometimes cutting, often amusing, was reserved for her extensive private diaries, and was not something she wished to publish in full.

How I wish she had shown me the diaries when I visited her tiny home, Pond Cottage, at Badminton, in her later years. I would love to have published them, even if shortened, in *Horse and Hound*. It is galling that I never saw the wonderfully delicate colour illustrations she added to her text, a talent reminiscent of the Edwardian England into which she was born. Merlin Unwin Books are to be congratulated on giving full rein to these beautiful works in this new biography.

We shall never experience again the unspoilt rural Britain, and its traditional hound sports, in the form which Daphne Moore loved and recorded with such devotion. I predict this story of her life will be increasingly valued as a fascinating sporting and social document, and it will entertain and inform today's lovers of hounds and their true place in our countryside.

Michael Clayton 2018

CHAPTER ONE

Who was Daphne Moore?

My own memories of Daphne Moore go back to the 1960s, when she could be seen following the Duke of Beaufort's hounds almost every day they hunted, usually arriving on a large, iron-framed, 'sit up and beg' bicycle of ancient vintage and, at every opportunity, taking to her feet.

A tall slim figure with an extremely cultured accent and possessing great poise, she followed hounds wearing a headscarf and tweed jacket. In the summer months she would be seen at the ringside of every hound show and most major puppy shows, writing a report for *Horse & Hound*.

Always well-dressed, with a smart hat, looking through lorgnettes at her catalogue, nothing would distract her concentration. Here was a lady who had become the greatest expert on foxhounds and their pedigrees of her day. Indeed, the 10th Duke of Beaufort, in his foreword to *The Book of the Foxhound*, the standard work on foxhound breeding, which she wrote in 1964, said:

"I know of no-one who takes a greater interest in foxhounds than the author of this book. In the field, in kennels, or on an occasion such as Peterborough Foxhound Show, Daphne Moore keeps her eye on the

Just half a dozen of Daphne Moore's many hunting diaries acquired by Michael O'Reilly in 2016 from Simon Hart MP and Chairman of Countryside Alliance, who had been left them by Daphne on her death in 2004. Simon has written the Foreword to this book.

hounds in view, and nothing will distract her attention from watching their progress. She is, too, a good judge of hounds, but it is in their pedigrees that I class her today with Mr Isaac Bell as the two greatest experts of our generation."

So how did Daphne Moore, author and journalist, come to occupy this exalted position of respect in the hunting world?

It certainly wasn't that she came from a privileged background which would have provided time and money for her to follow her passion for hunting.

In fact she was brought up in very straitened circumstances, managing to follow hounds by bicycling many miles to meets, travelling on trains and buses, and getting lifts from well-wishers whenever she could. She only rode to hounds in pre-war days when she was given horses to ride by Harry Gittins, a member of the extensive horse dealing and showing family, who was always pleased to find someone capable of riding the many horses that passed through his hands.

In the ten years leading up to the Second World War, she fox hunted almost every day throughout the winter and followed the otterhounds throughout the summer. During this time she spent a staggering total of 700 days foxhunting and 648 days otterhunting – and all on a shoestring. Even more remarkably, she wrote a detailed annual hunting diary for every day's otterhunting and another for every day's foxhunting. These were inscribed in her tiny but immaculate handwriting, peppered with literary quotations and poetry, and illustrated with exquisite, miniature, coloured pen and ink drawings.

I have quoted freely from these diaries in this book and we have reproduced many of her illustrations. The diaries start in 1930, when she was 20 years old, the final otterhunting diary being in 1950, with the foxhunting diaries continuing until 1960. Those written during the war are also of great interest, describing her life working in kennels, as a 'land girl' and on the famous Overbury Stud. Her later life

3

is well documented through her books and articles.

In 1976 Daphne wrote an article for *Shooting Times and Country* magazine entitled 'An Escapist Journal'. It began:

"For more than 20 years it was my practice, and immense pleasure, to keep a diary. They start exclusively as a hunting diary, profusely illustrated with minuscule sketches and countless photographs. During the war it developed into a general and natural history record of day-to-day proceedings, overshadowed inevitably by the war, but an example of escapism almost unrivalled!"

After "revisiting" a section of her 1942 diary, she finished by saying *"how merciful"* it was *"to have such endearing country sights and sounds 34 years later – and how vital that we cherish and preserve them."*

I hope that is what we have done in this book.

A 1957 cover of Horse and Hound showing Her Majesty the Queen admiring the Heythrop hounds with their Joint Master and huntsman, Captain Ronnie Wallace.
Note the price at 10 pence. Daphne wrote for Horse and Hound throughout her life.

This is a typical illustration which Daphne would paint in watercolour at the start of many entries in her diaries. How she had the energy and discipline to devote to these thirty or so meticulously-kept accounts of hunting days after her strenuous journey, often on bike, to get to the start of a hunt, to follow it on foot all day, to write her account for a newspaper or journal and then to keep her own diary for pleasure, is truly remarkable.

A selection of Daphne Moore's hunting diaries marked for inclusion in this book, meticulously kept over a period of 30 years and including her own charming marginal illustrations throughout.

Her diaries are not only a social commentary of her times and of the pre-war heydays of otterhunting, but are also full of detail of the characters, many of them legends of the hunting world, who have shaped the development of the modern foxhound.

The diaries tell us more about her character than her published articles and books. Those of us who remember her as a somewhat austere character in her later years may be surprised that the pre-war otterhunting diaries in particular show, not only how perceptive she was about people, but her sharp wit and, above all, her sense of fun.

They also highlight the enormous influence that George, 10th Earl of Coventry, Master of both the

The opening page of one of Daphne's diaries. Losing a number of close hunting friends in World War II makes her choice of this Rupert Brooke extract all the more poignant.

Croome Foxhounds and Hawkstone Otterhounds, had on the young Daphne. He clearly recognised the quite extraordinary enthusiasm of this young lady for hounds and hunting and helped her, whenever possible, to get to meets, passing on his views on the breeding of hounds and the value of the Welsh foxhound in particular. These were lessons she never forgot and he became her mentor and, in many ways, the father figure she had never known. Despite his death early in the war, she carried his convictions for the rest of her life.

What money she earned was through her writing ability, from the reports of the doings of her local packs in the regional press in the early days, to the articles she submitted to *Horse & Hound* and the rest of the sporting press, as well as the very well-informed reports on the major hound shows and puppy shows that she wrote until late into her life.

As an impoverished gentlewoman, who lived by 'grace and favour' on the Duke of Beaufort's estate at Badminton for the second half of her life, she made a great contribution to foxhunting, and hunting in general, and she was one of the most remarkable personalities in the great field sport which she adored.

CHAPTER TWO

Family Background

The Moores were an old and influential Gloucestershire family. They originated from a Worcester tanner of the early eighteenth century, whose son moved to Tewkesbury to pursue the same trade. Since then, Tewkesbury has seen family members as merchants, tanners, newspaper proprietors and politicians. In the mid 1800s Benjamin Moore, a solicitor, was appointed Her Majesty's Coroner – a position that remained in the family for over a hundred years.

Daphne Moore's great-grandfather, George Moore, was an eminent London surgeon before coming back to the small Cotswold market town of Moreton-in-Marsh to enable him to combine his medical duties with his passion for foxhunting.

His son John, also a doctor, but able to afford assistants to run the medical practice, was an even more passionate foxhunter, who married a local girl, Anne, with similar interests. They were both bold riders to hounds, hunting three or four days a week with the Heythrop, North Cotswold and Warwickshire, who all met within hacking distance of the town. We now see the strong hunting gene which paved the way for Daphne's lifelong love and commitment to hunting.

Ann Moore's addiction to hunting was probably the reason for her refusal to bear the usual large family of those days. She produced two daughters, one of which was Daphne's mother, Georgina, but always knows as Ina. She and her sister were born into a life of privilege, being educated by a succession of resident governesses before Ina attended Cheltenham Ladies College for just one year in her late teens.

Ina lived at home, her life revolving around the management of her parents' house, Warneford, when they went hunting. She herself was a nervous rider and followed the hounds by bicycle when they met nearby. She had a fine, professionally-trained, singing voice and was in great demand to sing on social occasions, including at some of the grand London houses during the season. But so it was that she found herself still a spinster at thirty years of age.

However, her circumstances changed on the death of her father only months into retirement. There was little money in his estate; Warneford House had to be sold and they moved to much smaller accommodation, denying them the trappings of their previous lifestyle.

At the same time, Ina's second cousin, Cecil Moore, considered a confirmed bachelor at the age of forty three, was negotiating the purchase of one of the grandest residences in Tewkesbury, Tudor House, which was in need of complete renovation and a woman's touch to oversee the internal refurbishment. Less than a year after Ina's father died, Cecil proposed and, following a brief engagement, Cecil and Ina were married in Tewkesbury Abbey in July 1905. However, Tudor House was proving to be a much more

Cecil Moore, Daphne's father, who died in 1918 at the age of 56.

Tudor House as it is today, the Tudor House Hotel in Tewkesbury. Daphne had lived here from only a few months old until she was seven, when the family had to sell up following the death and near-bankruptcy of her father Cecil.

costly and extensive project than Cecil had anticipated, so the newlyweds started life in rented accommodation, firstly at Uplands, an attractive Georgian house standing on Mythe Hill, and later at a smaller house near Tewkesbury Abbey, where Daphne was born in 1910.

Her elder brother John had been born at Uplands in 1907. Cecil worked in the family business of Moore & Sons, auctioneers and Estate Managers of Tewkesbury, and Ina undertook the management of the refurbishment of Tudor House. With a full staff of cook, lady's maid and general servant, she was able to entertain regularly, sing in the Abbey choir, receive daily communion and indulge her love of literature.

However, having miscarried her first child eleven months after marriage, after John's uneventful birth

Daphne and her brother John in 1912.

"We went to live there when I was only a few months old and John himself nearing his third birthday. It was an enchanting house for children, with queer old attics and a day-nursery which was panelled in old oak, and which had deep window seats from which we could look out on to the main street and watch all the dramas which were enacted there; in those days Tewkesbury was a backwater, with traffic at a minimum and that principally horse-drawn. In the gutter of what is now a busy thoroughfare little boys played marbles, there were Punch and Judy shows and many a barrel organ with the organ grinder's monkey dressed up in a miniature suit, seated on top. Once, on a never-to-be-forgotten occasion, I actually saw a dancing bear in the main street, walking upright beside its master. It was, I suppose, a brown bear; probably the last of its kind ever to be seen in Tewkesbury."

Ina became increasingly neurotic about his health and over the years her over-protective behaviour undoubtedly affected the upbringing of both John and Daphne. In addition, Cecil's health was also failing. Before they moved to Tudor House he had been taken ill and had had a tumour removed even before Daphne was born. It was five years after their marriage that the family finally moved into Tudor House, which was a fine example of Tewkesbury's original architectural splendour, constructed of timber in 1546. Daphne's earliest recollections are of life in Tudor House:

Daphne and John as young teenagers.

Both John and Daphne's early education came from their current nanny or nursery governess. Indeed, a wet-nurse, Nanny Brick, had been engaged when John was only three days old and, not unnaturally, he formed a close attachment to this matronly woman and adopted her broad Gloucestershire accent, necessitating her summary dismissal when he was three years old and the arrival of a governess of more genteel birth. Mary, who was well spoken, intelligent and reliable, and the next governess, Elizabeth, were both to have an important influence on Daphne's early education. The Moore family settled into a comfortable existence at Tudor House, little knowing the severe disruptions that would change their lives altogether within a few years.

On the outbreak of war in 1914, Ina dedicated herself to voluntary work and

The semi-detached council house at The Gastons, on the Gloucester Road, Tewkesbury, where Daphne and her mother were forced by circumstances to live – an enormous contrast to the grandeur of Tudor House. Daphne lived here without complaint until her mother's death in 1958, when she moved to Badminton.

Daphne aged 15 with her dog Bobs, taken at Barton House, Tewkesbury, which they briefly rented.

gave little time to the children or other domestic responsibilities and therefore did not anticipate the financial crisis that suddenly hit the family. Tudor House had exhausted Cecil's money and in 1917 they moved back to the Uplands, with minimal staff, while Ina organised the alteration of Tudor House into rented apartments. Cecil had never recovered from his original abdominal surgery and, after a rapid decline, he died in February 1918. Tewkesbury Abbey was packed for his funeral and there was much sympathy for the tall, elegant widow with a child on each hand who followed the coffin.

That very afternoon Ina was made aware of the severity of her financial position. Cecil had left £100 to his dear wife "in gratitude for her care". There

were no other funds and Tudor House carried a large mortgage. Cecil's shares in the business, furniture and silver and sale of Tudor House for £1,800, paid the mortgage and outstanding builders' accounts. Within a few years Tudor House became a hotel and remains so today.

Ina now relied on income from a £3,000 trust fund set up by her father and had to adapt to a lifestyle

Daphne's brother John with Bobs at Barton House on the same day in the summer of 1925.

Brother John at the time he was working for his uncle in the family business of Moore and Sons, Auctioneers and Estate Managers – before he left to become a full-time writer.

she had never experienced before. Initially she moved to Cheltenham, where her priority was to provide the children with an education and, with the assistance of relatives, she managed to fund the fees for a small private day school. However her irrational attitude towards the slightest illness kept both children at home more than at school and Tom Moore, Ina's brother-in-law, insisted that John be sent away to The Elms, which is still a well-known preparatory school near Malvern, and then to Malvern College.

Daphne aged 16, with brother John and mother Ina in 1926.

the address was No.11 Gastons. Ina lived here with Daphne for the rest of her life until she died in 1958. Always well turned out, she remained well-known in Tewkesbury, addressed as 'Mrs Cecil', due to the number of other Mrs Moores in the town. She was always well liked and respected for her continuing charitable work, visits to the sick and distribution of small kindnesses. Daphne remembers:

"She was the most important influence of our young lives for, as a widow after only thirteen years of marriage, she had all the responsibility of bringing us up. She spoiled us unashamedly and unashamedly we adored her for it."

It was then that Ina suggested that she also move to Malvern "to educate the children" and Daphne was sent to Malvern Girls College. However, finances would not permit John to remain at Malvern College beyond the age of sixteen and Daphne was delighted that after "these years of exile" they returned to their native Tewkesbury as soon as possible. Her schooling continued at Tewkesbury High School.

Reality now really set in and the family moved to a semi-detached council house on the Gloucester Road

The Moore relations who had no doubt invested in the education of the children in order that John should join the family business must have been disappointed when, after only three years as a junior in the firm, he announced that he wanted to become a writer. His uncle, the senior partner, famously responded: *"A writer; that's a hobby my boy, not a profession."* It is interesting that both John and Daphne's only income for the rest of their lives came from writing. Daphne's diaries contain endless quotes from a wide selection of poets. Her interest and knowledge of literature and poetry were undoubtedly encouraged by her "elocution mistress" at Malvern Girls College who was *"imaginative enough to allow us eleven-year-olds to choose works from any of the poets to recite in class. I chose one of John's poems and stood up proudly to declaim 'Ode to a Trout', by John C. Moore, a performance which was still recalled by that elocution teacher forty years on"*.

John Moore of course became Gloucestershire's best-known and loved author of the twentieth century. He wrote some 40 books, had a regular column in the *Birmingham Evening Mail* for 18 years, and was a familiar broadcaster on radio. Most of his work drew on his deep knowledge as a countryman and naturalist, which manifested itself in his novels. He was a true conservationist as well as a country sportsman. He was responsible for starting the Cheltenham Literary Festival in 1949, when he became Honorary Artistic Director, a post he held for many years.

Despite his successes, his life was a roller coaster of financial crisis, but his memory lives on through the John Moore Countryside Museum, opened by his friend Ludovic Kennedy in 1980, and the John Moore Society, which produces a journal twice a year and holds regular lectures and social events.

Daphne's mother Ina, a widow after only 13 years of marriage.

John Moore with his wife Lucile and mother Ina at his house, Lower Mill Farm, Kemerton, in the 1950s.

Ina Moore (1873–1958) in later life.

or loved the countryside more deeply. He realised that the glorious patchwork of little fields and woodland owed their origin to the men who had created and maintained uneconomic copses and spinneys as cover for pheasants and foxes."

John Moore (1907–1967), who became one of Gloucestershire's best-known and loved authors of the twentieth century. He wrote some 40 books, had a regular column in the Birmingham Evening Mail for 18 years, and was a familiar broadcaster on radio.

When she was aged 77, Daphne produced and introduced an anthology of her brother's work entitled *Sport and the English Countryside – the world of John Moore*, with a foreword by Phil Drabble, the well-known broadcaster on country matters and host of *One Man and his Dog* on television.

Phil Drabble wrote: *"John Moore belonged to what is now an endangered species of 'Sportsman-Naturalist'. He loved fishing and shooting and, as a boy, he was an avid collector of butterflies, all of which are frowned on by fashionable conservationists today! But nobody was a truer countryman*

CHAPTER THREE

Halcyon Pre-War Days

Daphne started her remarkable hunting diaries, both foxhunting and otterhunting, in 1930 when she was twenty years old and during those ten years that preceded the war there were not many days that she did not go hunting. Living in the small house at the Gastons, she remembers that her mother soon became resigned to her absence four and five days a week all the year round.

At that time, the boundaries of three foxhound packs converged on the town of Tewkesbury – the Croome, Cotswold and Ledbury –

whilst "Collie" Unwin's Arle Court Harriers were kennelled nearby and the Wye Valley Otterhounds provided summer sport.

Daphne's earliest diary entry was April 12th 1930 with the Wye Valley Otterhounds from Bourton village, when she took the bus to Cheltenham, where she got a lift with friends. It was not a memorable day, but Daphne was already showing her keen interest in the hounds, noting:

"The hounds were already there when we arrived, and about half a dozen new hounds

The Hawkstone Otterhounds move off from Croome Park in May 1936, led by kennel-huntsman Bill Porter and the whipper-in, followed by the Master, Lord Coventry, who hunted hounds.

had been bought from the Harriers and Foxhounds, but several of the old hounds had gone. Poor old Bouncer died during the winter and Wycombie has been put down, but Woodman, Singer, Whynot and most of the best old hounds are still going strong."

Her first morning with the foxhounds, with the Croome from Eckington on August 25th, was no more memorable, but she writes:

"I started off from Tewkesbury on my bicycle at about 5.45 this morning – the alarm clock

The Lygon girls out cubhunting wearing flannels, much to Daphne's disapproval. "All very well for the sea, but for cubhunting – no!"

having gone off just before 5.00 and my breakfast finished soon after half past! It was a perfectly wonderful morning… no mist to speak of, and the sunrise over Bredon Hill was simply marvellous.”

Her notes on some of the characters, however, are remarkably succinct…

“A young man and maiden who had arrived at the first covert (he was presumably an army man, judging from scraps of his conversation and his somewhat vacuous expression!) had also departed, and two of the Lygon girls, who had come out for a short time, attired most weirdly in long flannel trousers – all very well for the sea, but for cubhunting – no!”

One gets the impression that sport with the Croome in those early days was of a fairly pedestrian nature, but that was all about to change with the Mastership of George 10th Earl of Coventry, who became Daphne's idol and mentor and shaped her views on foxhounds for ever. George Coventry came to his inheritance at Croome in 1931, bringing with him a small private pack of Carmarthenshire hounds, of which he had been previously Master.

He hunted this pack by invitation of the Croome and the Worcestershire that season before becoming Joint Master of his family pack, the Croome, the following year. For a time the two packs remained in separate kennels, the

Croome bitches at Kinnersley, only a mile away, while Lord Coventry continued to keep his hounds at Croome Court, along with the Hawkstone Otterhounds of which he was also Master. The Coventrys were very good to Daphne, often giving her a lift to the meets, particularly to those of the otterhounds, which were often some distance away in Wales. She still followed the foxhounds on foot or bicycle.

Lord Coventry hunting the Hawkstone Otterhounds on the river Ithon in 1936. He brought many of these hounds from the Carmarthenshire Foxhounds, where he was previously Master.

A wartime meet of the Hawkstone Otterhounds in 1940 with their new Deputy Master and huntsman, Ronnie Wallace on the right and Joint Master Pip Stanier behind.

Daphne was now hunting correspondent for the Croome for the local newspaper at a penny a line. She therefore particularly appreciated members of the field with double-barrelled surnames, which could be worth at least a halfpenny each! She soon graduated to the columns of *Horse and Hound*, writing under the pseudonym of "Tally-Ho" with the foxhounds and the corresponding otterhunting term of "Heu-Gaze" with the Hawkstone.

She wrote for *Horse and Hound* for well over fifty years.

George Coventry was one of a group of influential Masters, led by the American, "Ikey" Bell, and including Sir Peter Farquhar, the Duke of Beaufort, Bill Scott, Cyril Heber-Percy, Jack Evans (of the Brecon) and other far-sighted Masters who were concerned that the 'fashionable' type of hound that was winning at Peterborough had become too heavy and lacked activity. They favoured a hound with a lighter frame and good shoulders, which would run up with the pack for more seasons. They achieved their object by crossing their hounds with the Welsh, and Sir Edward Curre in south Wales had been doing this for some time, as had George Coventry at the Carmarthenshire. The hounds that he brought to the Croome from Wales were more the type of the present day foxhound than those in the majority of kennels in the 1930s.

Lord Coventry's little Carmarthenshire-bred pack finished their first cubhunting season from Croome in 1932 with an outstanding hunt. Daphne was not out, but, at the formal Croome Opening Meet two days later she records:

"Everyone is talking about a simply marvellous hunt which Lord Coventry's hounds had last Thursday at Naunton Beauchamp. I am broken-hearted at having missed it, as if I could have got there, probably Mr Ewins from the Wheelbarrow & Castle

Daphne with Donne, Lady Coventry, at a meet of the Croome at Beckford, Lord Coventry behind.

would have given me a lift and he was with them all the time.

They found at Naunton Bushes and pulled their fox down in the open after 1¾ hours, with an eight-mile point and sixteen miles as hounds ran. Every hound was up at the finish. John told me all about it last night and Lyes started to tell me again this morning – I do wish I'd been there. There were only about seven people out. I imagine those who didn't go are cursing themselves! This will make the people who run down the "Welsh" hounds sit up a bit!"

These hounds were not Welsh in the pure sense of the word, but a skilful blend of the best of the old Welsh and English strains. However, the fact that these hounds' pedigrees did not contain all pure English Stud Book hounds, caused deep divisions within the foxhunting world and they were of course not eligible for the Stud Book themselves. It was not until 1955 that the *Foxhound Kennel Stud Book* was 'opened' thanks to the influence of Sir Peter Farquhar.

The Hawkstone Otterhounds at Croome Court, the Coventrys' home, in 1936. Hounds are led by kennel-huntsman, Bill Porter, and the whipper-in, followed by the Master and huntsman, Lord Coventry, and Daphne Moore, who whipped-in that day.

This photograph is captioned in Daphne's diary as "otterhunters at play!" It shows Daphne on the beach at Llangrannog, Cardigan Bay, in July 1936.

Daphne's foxhunting was revolutionised when, in 1934, Harry Gittins came to live in Worcestershire, only a few miles from the Croome kennels. As a farmer and horse dealer he had a great many horses through his hands which he needed to get out hunting to find out their capabilities and show them to prospective customers. It is remarkable, and great testament to Daphne's pluck and courage, that, as someone who had only learnt to ride on friends' ponies' as a child, she now thought nothing of riding over twenty different horses in a season, many of them very young and green. But, as she says: "Good or bad, it was the purest joy to me in those days to be on anything with four legs". All other days she would rely on her own two legs and her bicycle, although her first bicycle fell apart after being consistently rough–ridden across country and was finally sold to the scrap merchant for four pence!

George Coventry's private pack continued to impress. As Daphne noted:

Daphne at lunch with hounds near Soudley with the Wye Valley Otterhounds in 1930.

"Those Carmarthenshire-bred hounds were terrors to hunt and could do so with the minimum of human aid."

In February 1934 they bought off a remarkable hunt in the rough country near the north-western boundary of their territory.

"The ferry-boat at Pixham, instead of being stuck in the mud as it was last year when needed for this meet, was sunk last week, which complicated things considerably. Eventually, hounds had to be sent by train from Defford to Knightwick with Fred, *and Bill to help him, as neither John nor Harry were out. The Master took Lyes (the terrierman) and myself in the Chrysler as far as Knightwick Station, where he had hounds and horses unloaded, and rode on to the meet at Alfrick – a bit late, but he had rung up everyone he could think of to tell them of the delay."*

During a difficult scenting morning, when several foxes were hunted, Daphne writes: *"I tried to learn their notes – I really think I know Lexicon's now, but am very bad at learning their*

Hawkstone Sinbad, a Welsh-cross hound, in June 1930.

voices. I'd love to be able to tell them all apart like the Master."

A fox from High Wood in the Croome country was quickly away and hounds were out of sight before Daphne and the other foot followers could climb the bank to get a view. Despite looking everywhere, that was the last they saw of them:

"I wish I had gone on, but it was too late now to do anything but await their return and cogitate upon the wonderful run they must be having. At last, about 4 o'clock, we heard the Master's horn near Knightwick and I walked with Lyes down to the station, but they had not yet arrived, so I started to walk to meet them. They soon came in to sight – the Master, Fred and a man on a chestnut cob – Mr Pope I believe. As we went back to the station the Master told me what they had done and what a hunt it must have been! From the coalpits they made for Suckley (North Ledbury),

A CROOME ALPHABET.

A is Tom Andrews, the famed Gin-and-Beer   B is for Bomford, a sporting old dear

C is for Chatham, both father and son; D is for Death, selling coal by the ton (MR. LYSTER OF CHELTENHAM)

E is for Essle, a Colonel at that; F is for Freddy,   flirtatious and fat ("FREDDY SLADE, Sir Alfred Slade)

G is for Gresson, so courtly and kind; H is for Hundy, who plods on behind

I is Impossible, nothing to say; J is John Coventry   riding his grey

K is for Kenneth, the Hunt Secretary; L's Lygons, Dorothy,   Sybell   and Mary

M is our Masters   the best ever bred; N is too our ever-popular Ned;

O is for "Ossie" (or Captain D. Smith); P is for Pye, whose reports are all myth;

Q is Quartette viz: the Lygons and Jo; R's Forbra's trainer — Tom Rimell, you know;

S is for Slade, and also for Statter; T is for Tiger,   as mad as a hatter;

U is for Unwin, who loves horse and hound; V is for Vic,   a good terrier to ground;

W's Jack Willis — he's viewed: "Gone away."

X is the X-tra-ordin'ry way

Diana's hair   changes   from day to day   (DIANA COVENTRY)

Y and Z can't be rhymed, so they finish my lay.

"A Croome Alphabet", written and illustrated by Daphne and depicting various members of the Hunt.

went over the road to Bringsty Common and past Brockhampton to Bradley Wood and Tedstone Delamere (North Hereford). Then on past Clifton (Clifton on Teme) to Tedney when they killed just short of the wood.

The country is just frightful to ride over, with wire everywhere, and this meant sticking to bye-roads, so that the Master was half an hour behind hounds at Tedney. He was met by a farmer who led him to the spot where they had killed and showed him the remains

– which were few, as they had broken him up well. They had run at terrific speed for some forty-five minutes, touching no less than four hunt countries and making a point of about seven and a half miles – more as hounds ran."

The following season, with George Coventry as sole Master, Daphne stayed at Croome Court for the first two mornings' cubhunting and a couple of days' otterhunting with the Hawkstone, of which George Coventry was also Master and Huntsman. On August 22nd the Hawkstone met at Caer Beris, on that lovely tributary of the Wye, the river Irfon, where a brace were accounted for. Daphne came back to Croome Court with the Master and the secretary of the Hawkstone, Pip Stanier. The next morning Daphne writes:

"Yesterday I went with the Master and Pip down to Caer Beris, near Builth Wells hunting the otter, and came back to Croome last night to stay till Saturday for two morning's cubhunting and another day's otterhunting, which is just heavenly.

This morning Alfred called me at about 4.45, when it was still pitch dark, and after breakfast George and Donne [Lady Coventry] went round to the stables to get their horses and Pip and the children and myself started across to the Boat House Covert, which was to be the first draw. There was a heavy mist and one couldn't see more than about 25 yards at this time of the morning, though by 7.00 it had quite cleared.

We waited outside the covert for five minutes or so, and could hear the hounds in kennel lifting up their voices in lamentation at being left behind – then we heard hounds entering the covert on the far side and Pavitt rating a puppy. It was all silent for a second or so, then, a dash in to covert and a great burst of music from the pack and George's voice cheering them on. He had an awful dream the other night in which all his hounds had suddenly become mute and on the first cubbing morning hunted without any cry whatsoever. This terrible nightmare was far from being fulfilled, for, as usual with these hounds there was magnificent music, even though more than half the pack was composed of puppies – 23 couple of hounds, 12½ being puppies."

During a busy morning, Daphne reports:

"Joan swore that she saw one of the Committee's hounds with the rest in covert, and it turned out that she was perfectly right, for old Willing, who is loose in the kennel yard with her puppies, decided to stroll across and join the fun. She thoroughly enjoyed it too! I have learnt some of the puppies, but still have a great many more to know, and am going to get them off by heart before embarking on the bitch pack."

The following day the Hawkstone met at Pont-a'r–ithon on the river Ithon and Daphne's diary notes:

"We had a heavenly morning's cubhunting with the Welsh pack yesterday from the kennels and little Rocket caught a cub in the lake to finish up with. They had hunted him well and truly for over an hour, finding in Menagerie and had him dead beat by the time he took to water. Today we started from Croome at 8.00, four of us, George and Pip, Donne and myself, to say nothing of Mr Knox."

Daphne riding Ebb-Tide, one of Harry Gittins' horses, pictured outside his house at Clifton Court Farm.

Hounds immediately struck a drag (the scent of the otter's movements overnight), which continued all day, with hounds hunting really strongly at times with a great cry, but without working up to their quarry. However, it is worth noting the physical reality of following otterhounds all day as described by Daphne on this occasion:

"The walking here is extremely difficult, for on the left hand is an impenetrable jungle, and to cross to the other bank one is forced to wade through deep water, over slippery, treacherous stones on the river bottom, contending at the same time with a very violent current. George, Pip and Harry crossed at a rather deep and very dangerous ford, which so petrified me when I began to follow that I made for a better place lower down and was therefore left a long way behind and had to run to catch up with hounds."

Having described the rest of the day, she concluded:

"We reached Croome just in time to change for dinner, finding Gerry there before us. We were very Hawkstone at dinner tonight, George and Pip both being in their H.O.H. dinner jackets and Gerry resplendent in his H.O.H. tails."

So Daphne's life continued at this time of year, foxhunting and

These early diaries show a lighter side of Daphne Moore, having fun and laughter with her sometimes chivalrous otterhunting companions.

The shadow of the war and its impact on the hunt and on Daphne's friends had not yet been felt.

otterhunting claiming most of her days. She would leave home on her bicycle in the dark at five or six o'clock in the morning to collect a horse from Harry Gittins and then hack up to ten miles to go cubhunting. If no horse was available she would follow by bicycle and on foot and, wherever possible, go on to hunt with the otterhounds for the rest of the day.

Daphne Moore (fourth from left in front row) with fellow followers and huntsmen of the Wye Valley otterhounds at a meet at Hampton, Evesham in the mid-1930s.

CHAPTER FOUR

Further Pre-War Hunting

While the Croome remained the "home" pack for Daphne, the Ledbury usually met within bicycling distance on Fridays and the Cotswold hunted the vale near Tewkesbury on Tuesdays. This was considered the cream of the country then, but, since the war, when the Cotswold decided that they could no longer afford to hunt so many days, this vale has been hunted by the Cotswold Vale Farmers and is now sadly bisected by the M5 motorway.

The Arle Court Harriers were kennelled within a mile of Daphne's home and were the private pack of Mr "Collie" Unwin, maintained entirely at the Master's expense, with no subscription or cap taken and hunting hares only.

In 1933 Collie Unwin recorded his one-thousandth day hunting hounds and on non-hunting days rode out with neighbouring foxhounds. He became a great friend of Daphne's and would ring her every Tuesday and Saturday evening to discuss the day's sport with the Croome. His nephew, Tim Unwin, was a distinguished Master of the Cotswold for over 30 years, hunting hounds from 1971, and breeding a top class pack.

Collie Unwin, longtime Master and huntsman of his own private pack, the Arle Court Harriers, pictured with his hounds at Southwick Park in 1936.

It is Daphne's first diary that records the formation of the British Field Sports Society. It started with a decision taken at the Annual General Meeting of the Devon and Somerset Staghounds, held at Taunton in May 1930, to form a society for the protection of all field sports. Daphne, like most hunting supporters at that time, received a letter from the Chairman of the proposed organisation, Lord Bayford, asking for her support "by her membership and influence". It was counter-signed by many of the great and the good of the West Country hunting world.

A further letter, dated 27th November 1930 announced the first meeting of the British Field Sports Society to be held at the Caxton Hall, Westminster, at 3pm on Thursday, 4th December, 1930 where the Duke of Beaufort had consented to preside.

The Devon and Somerset had donated one hundred pounds to cover preliminary expenses. The minimum subscription was fixed at one shilling per annum "in order that anyone may join the Society who desires to do so" and it was estimated that the income produced would "be sufficient to ensure that the work of the Society may proceed unhampered by any financial worries." Daphne Moore subscribed five shillings that first year and of course the BFSS, which developed into the Countryside Alliance in 1997 has been working in the promotion and defence of field sports ever since.

Cubhunting with the Ledbury in 1931, Daphne noted that *"the mixed pack were out and Bob Champion, of course, was hunting them. He has a very deep noted horn, rather nice, and far preferable to the squeaky thing used by Collie Unwin with the Harriers."*

In December 1931 Lord Coventry, still hunting his private pack by invitation of the Croome at this stage, had written Daphne's telephone number and address on the back of his matchbox, promising to let her know next time his hounds were meeting nearby. Daphne has kept the card he sent her:

"I received this this morning and had to pay a penny on it owing to the Victorian stamp! Evidently it is one of the old Lord Coventry's cards which he used when he started the Croome, which went by the name of Lord Coventry's Hounds until the year 1882. At the meet four days later, I thanked Lord Coventry for his card and he asked me if the stamp worked. I had to tell him it didn't!"

The Opening Meet of the Wye Valley Otterhounds at Usk in April 1938. Daphne with her otterhunting pole in centre and the celebrated Master and huntsman of the Wye Valley, Ray Williams, on the right.

Above: Bolting an otter from a tangled mass of driftwood at the Hawkstone Opening Meet in 1938.
Below: a detail from Daphne's diary showing a similar scene on the Teme.

Daphne's enthusiasm for Welsh-cross hounds soon brought her into contact with Bill Scott, who had come to the North Cotswold as Master in 1932. He had already made his name at the Portman and, after the war, was to hunt the West Waterford, the Portman again as Joint Master with Sir Peter Farquhar, and finally the Old Berks. His son Martin later hunted the

LEINTWARDINE.

(On the Little Teme.)

so many dogs, and more men, all in pursuit of the Otter."

Tiverton and the V.W.H. which he has continued to breed as the leading expert on hound pedigrees today. But back to March 1934 when Daphne notes:

"Instead of going to the Berkeley Arms with the Croome bitches today, I decided to take a busman's holiday and go to Toddington to have a look at the North Cotswold. My chief reason for this was that Mr Scott, their Master, has just sent his best bitch to Verdict and, I hear, has a lot of Welsh-crosses already in his pack. All of which rather thrilled me and I was longing to see them. Having missed the meet, I had a word with the whip later in the day and he told me that the bitch has gone to Croome – her name is Lively. I do hope her puppies will be Verdict-y ones."

After a hard day when she rode her bicycle across country, getting it bogged in several gateways, and pushing it to the top of Stanway Hill,

Pip Stanier hunting hounds in 1938. Daphne second from right.

It was August 1936 when Daphne first came across Ronnie Wallace as the young Master and huntsman of the Eton College Beagles. His parents had taken a house at Bishop's Cleeve, near Cheltenham, on a short lease and the beagles were to be kennelled there for the summer and Christmas holidays. She noted that:

she concluded: *"The wind was against me all the way back to Tewkesbury and I had great difficulty in getting along."*

"Ron and the professional K-H wear brown velvet coats and hunting caps and white breeches – all of which must be very hot in

Kennel-huntsman of the Hawkstone, Bill Porter, with the famous Airedale/Foxhound cross, Airman.

Daphne (right) enjoys a picnic with friends at the Carmarthen Show, 1937.

the middle of the summer! It was a scorching day and I wore the absolute minimum of clothes, but found it terribly hot running all the same. It's a beautiful level-looking pack and the hounds are much smaller than I expected – 15 inches only."

The young Wallace hunted these beagles for two seasons and Daphne's best day with them was on Christmas Eve the following season from Cleeve Grange when she remembers:

"This morning I bicycled over to Bishops Cleeve by 11.30 and left my bike at the Lodge. Vivian (Ronnie Wallace's brother) had to go to Cheltenham and wasn't whipping-in, so, to my huge delight, Ron

asked me to take a whip. It's always so much more interesting to hunt with any sort of hounds if one has a job of work to do."

During the first good hunt she wrote with her usual humour:

"At one point I saw the Loch Ness Monster lying flat on his front on the grass and thought that he was having a heart attack or else had tripped up and sprained his ankle…but the next moment he was on his feet, with his cap held high in the air. He had merely viewed the hare, and, like the ostrich, had imagined that he was making himself invisible!"

Later in the day, drawing again,

"Ron told me to go on to the far side of the spinney, and no sooner had he thrown hounds in than I viewed a big, beautiful dog fox away. I warned Ron, and a second or so later, hounds hit off the line and they would have been away in a flash had not Perkins and I been on the far side to stop them. Perkins had previously seen a tired

hare going back over Kate Farm, where we originally found and now hounds put her up again, and, after hunting well and fast for a quarter of an hour, pulled her down in a thick fence. I had the mask, and, as it won't be possible to let the taxidermist have it before the Christmas holidays, I left it at the fishmongers on my way home, to go into cold storage until Wednesday!"*

The final hunt was particularly fast:

"There was scarcely a check all through this hunt, and I, who was getting pretty

Bill Perkins, kennel-huntsman of the Eton College Beagles from 1926 to 1949 with hounds by 'Pop' wall.

well beat, almost prayed for one now. But they caught her at the edge of a ploughed field behind Cleeve Grange, after a very rapid half-hour. I saw hounds fed and then went in to tea at Cleeve Grange – a most enormous one, with two eggs; and bicycled home in the dark."

Years later, Daphne recalls meeting Perkins, the kennel-huntsman at that time, at a Puppy Show and remarked that he looked just the same as he did when he whipped-in to Captain Wallace before the war. "Ah Miss", he replied, "I'm not the same; I never shall be the same again. He nearly KILLED me!"

The season 1938-39 was the peak of Daphne's foxhunting, when she had over one hundred days and rode twenty-two different horses. She hunted with the Croome, usually four days a week, the Cotswold, Ledbury,

Bay de Courcy-Parry, or 'Dalesman' to his readers in Horse and Hound, pictured at the Anchor Inn in Shropshire, which he bought 'in order to obtain a drink' while Master of the United Pack.

Worcestershire, South Hereford, Col. Spence-Colby's, North Shropshire, Berkeley and Mr de Courcy-Parry's (later to become the West Warwickshire). "Bay" de Courcy-Parry, better known as "Dalesman", his pseudonym when writing his many articles for *Horse and Hound*, was born before the turn of the century. He had fought in the First World War, but spent the rest of his life hunting numerous packs of hounds, both mounted and on foot, as a Master and as an honorary huntsman.

He was one of life's great characters and famously bought the Anchor Inn, while Master of the United Pack in Shropshire, because the landlord refused to open up during the afternoon as they hacked home after a long morning's cubhunting. The cheque for £700 which was pushed under the door would have bounced had Bay not rung his father that night and asked if he would care to invest in a hill farm. He recalls that his father seemed to lack the enthusiasm expected of him when he found the property was a public house.

Daphne remembers the day she whipped-in to Dalesman's little Clun Forest pack of beagles, hunting the Ledbury Vale by invitation *"Without doubt this was about the hardest day I have ever had with ANY hounds."*

Michael Lyne, the well-known sporting artist, who was a good friend of Daphne's, lived near Winchcombe in the Cotswold country, and formed a small

The young Ronnie Wallace, as Master of the Eton College Beagles, leads hounds over the road following a meet at the College in 1937.

private pack of beagles and "seagles" – the latter being a cross between a beagle and a Sealyham terrier.

In December 1938 Daphne bicycled, hitch-hiked and walked to their fixture at Tilesford Aerodrome, where they had been invited to meet. She reported that:

"Michael's pack is now reduced to 3½ couple which produced a very good day's beagling. The famous 'aerodrome hare' was killed handsomely after a splendid hunt, *whilst hounds accounted for another in the late afternoon after running all day."*

The following season of 1939-40 was very different as the war clouds gathered. Daphne had only 35 days' hunting, compared to over 100 the previous season. George Coventry had resigned his Mastership for the following season, but the committee eventually persuaded him to continue with Mr Marcus Stapleton Martin as a Joint Master, thus continuing the long association between the Coventry family and the Hunt.

Daphne writes:

"It is sad to think it is the end of the season – more particularly as the future is so terribly uncertain. I have loved this season's hunting, perhaps more than normal peace-time seasons, and I hate to feel that it is at an end."

CHAPTER FIVE

Otterhunting before the War

Daphne Moore has said that her 'Golden Age' – certainly as far as otterhunting was concerned – was the decade immediately preceding World War II. During those years she spent a total of 648 days otterhunting and must have walked many thousands of miles. She admits that, being a more leisurely and less serious form of hunting than foxhunting, it leads to a great deal of fun and good fellowship, which is so well described in her diaries.

Otterhunting is a much older sport than foxhunting, dating back some 800 years. Men who have hunted several of the quarry species all say that hunting the otter provides the purest form of hound work.

Daphne states that every true otter hunter is something of a naturalist at heart and much of the pleasure of otterhunting is derived from the fact that it usually takes place on some of the wildest and most beautiful rivers in the country. Few animals possess a scent which lies so long and thus the overnight movements of their quarry enable the hounds to hunt the "drag"

and work up to where it is lying. Thereafter, they are able to hunt it when it is under the water, also taking into account both the wind and the flow of the river.

In those pre-war days, of course, otters were plentiful and, long before the otter became a protected species, it was the otterhunters, in the 1960s, who rang the first alarm bells of its decline. The increasing use of crop sprays, which included dieldrin and DDT, were draining into the river systems and making the species infertile. At the same time, misguided and ignorant Animal Rights activists were releasing American mink from the fur farms. These foreign and vicious predators multiplied with great speed, causing chaos in the natural world and decimating much of the wildlife on our rivers, such as water voles, nesting water birds and of course otters. From the 1960s onwards, the otterhound packs voluntarily ceased to hunt their original quarry, changing instead to hunt the mink.

As a teenager, Daphne would go out with her brother John with the Wye Valley Otterhounds, who came to Tewkesbury twice a year for two or three consecutive days' hunting. However, as her brother's interest in the chase dwindled, hers soared, and it was not long before she was hunting with the Wye Valley more regularly and travelling further afield to hunt with them. Hounds were hunted by Joint Master, Ray Thompson, who was somewhat of a legend in the otterhunting world.

During the summer of 1930 the twenty-year-old Daphne expanded her otterhunting horizons by arranging a hunting holiday with her friend Mary, a niece of the legendary Master of the Hawkstone Otterhounds, Arthur Jones, who, at the same time, was Master of the Worcestershire Foxhounds. He

Daphne aged 20 outside her tent, with her terrier Bobs, while on her first otterhunting tour in June 1930.

had also formerly been Master and huntsman of the Northern Counties and Bucks Otterhounds successively. Young Daphne had met the great Arthur Jones on her first visit to the Hawkstone earlier that sumner and had noted *"the Master – Arthur Jones – wears a scarlet cap and coat, which hardly matches his rather lurid complexion!"*

However, she later described him *"with his little white terrier, James, he was a great character – the bluff, hearty, old type of otterhunter, blessed with a very kind heart hidden in that slightly crude exterior."*

Daphne and Mary set off on 22nd June.

"We (Mary and myself) started from Malvern yesterday morning in her Morris Oxford, packed to the brim with our suitcases, stoves, tent, etc, and arrived at our present camping ground late in the afternoon. It is at a farm just above a wee village called Ram, and is ideal, but for its nearness to the road. The farm people are extremely Welsh, but awfully kind to us, and we get our milk from them. Last night was rather stormy, but our tent is perfectly watertight and we slept fairly well. The view is wonderful. However, this is an otterhunting diary, so let's proceed to today's hunting. We met at Tregarron, beyond Lampeter, at 10.30 and drew down the Teifi, where hounds spoke once or twice to a drag, but did not find."

Arthur Jones, Master and huntsman of the Hawkstone Otterhounds when Daphne first hunted with them, pictured in 1930 with his famous terrier 'James the Great'.

However, in the afternoon:

"...having golluped our lunch (the Hawkstone very rarely have a lunch interval!) we caught hounds up further downstream. There was a pretty hot scent and hounds seemed very keen, scratching at the bank. There was a large Welshy crowd out, who were fearfully thrilled and when at last the otter was viewed their excitement

The Bucks Otterhounds meet at Beard Mill in August 1932.

knew no bounds! The hunt lasted for about ¾ of an hour and towards the end was most exciting. The Master gave me a pad, which bucked me considerably. The Master suspected there was another otter about, so put hounds in again and in a very short time hounds had found a second time and before long had killed a bitch this time. He has one particular hound – a cross between an Airedale and a Foxhound – whom he adores and who follows him always. His name is Airman and he is unequalled in tackling an otter.

When we reached our camp again we were met by the old dame who owns the farm, in great trouble, with tales of boys throwing stones at our tent, a gypsy nearly coming and lying on our beds, and things being pinched

Daphne's sketch of Airman, the famous Airedale/ Foxhound cross, a favourite of Arthur Jones, and unequalled as an otterhound.

from previous campers in the vicinity. Apparently she had been wanting to go and visit her sister in Ram, but had had to stay in all day to guard our tent and goods!

Consequently we have decided to move on tomorrow to Llandyssul, where hounds are staying and Harry (Harry Nicholas, first whipper-in and kennel huntsman) knows of a farm where we can camp."

The following day, after an early start, the two girls arrived at the meet of the Pembroke and Carmarthen at Abergwili, near Carmarthen, where hounds had a strong drag in the morning, later finding an otter on a

John Coventry, George Coventry's younger brother and Mayor of Worcester that year in 1930.

tributary of the Towy. The following morning they were out with the Hawkstone and it was memorable in that it was the first day that Daphne met the new Lord Coventry, who was at that time still Master of the Carmarthenshire Foxhounds and living in Wales.

"Mr Richardson took us to the meet this morning in his 20 h.p. Sunbeam Saloon – a topping car, far preferable to its owner. He came round to our camp last night, bothering us, and though we were both absolutely indifferent to him, stayed on talking for ages. Mary flicked the washing-up mop in his face once!

However, even though he is an objectionable creature, it's much nicer to be taken to the meet than to take the Morris, and drive round all the time. The Coventrys were at the meet – John Coventry (Mayor of Worcester that year) and the new Lord Coventry with Pip Stanier." [Honorary Secretary from 1930 to 1958 and Joint Master and huntsman for some years].

Not finding on the first stream, it was decided to van hounds to High Mead on the Teifi.

"Richardson's car was some way off and we would have had a good way to walk had we not got a lift on the running board of Dorothy Davis-Evans' car. It was pretty full up inside with herself and the Coventrys, and Pip Stanier in the dickey!

As soon as hounds started to draw the river they spoke to a fresh drag. The Master told Mary and myself to watch where a little backwater ran in to the main stream. Though we kept our eyes glued on it fairly continuously for about half-an-hour, the otter somehow managed to elude us and was hollered further downstream. Harry turned him, and hounds hunted him upstream again and he went up the little backwater and into the main river again further up.

There was a covert the opposite side to which we were standing and the otter made for this and was hunted on land for some little time, until eventually they caught him at the edge of the coppice, by the water. Pip Stanier caught hold of him and nearly lost the beautiful new cap he was wearing for the first time in doing so – the Master "christened" it for him by ducking it in the water!

Daphne riding the running board of Dorothy Davis-Evans' car, with the Coventrys as passengers and Pip Stanier in the dickey.

A meet of otterhounds in 1931.

*A break for lunch with the Hawkstone at Barrett's Mill, near Ludlow.
Left to right: Daphne, Lord Coventry, Mr and Mrs Berrington, the artist Michael Lyne and Pip Stanier,
Hunt secretary.*

It was a 17 or 18lb dog otter, and the hunt lasted nearly an hour I should think, and was quite an exciting one. Richardson has asked us to dinner at the Porth to-night, so we shall have it with the Master too. We shall have to wear respectable clothes for once!"

Two further days with the Hawkstone followed, the first on the Teifi being wet, but hounds hunted a screaming drag before Guardsman winded the otter up a ditch and caught it quickly.

The final Hawkstone day was from Lampeter Bridge, also on the Teifi, and proved to be the only blank day of their six-day week. *"There was a fearful crowd*

of people at the meet – chiefly small boys and village toughs, and Richardson had the time of his life trying to keep them from getting ahead of hounds! They didn't find, owing, so the Master said, to the crowd of hooligans who were out.

There was a priceless little raft made of board on four tubs, taking passengers across at High Mead, but Mary and I waded through, though we did find it rather deep on the far side. Richardson went across on the raft – it would have been marvellous to wreck it with him aboard!!" The girls then drove on north to Towyn and had three days with the Border Counties Otterhounds before they returned home. The Border Counties were hunted by David Jones – "a dear old Welshman, who has been with the hounds for over 30 years, since the age of 14! David uses such queer hound language "Brr – brr" he says, when Ray would say "Leu in there!"

They are a nice looking lot of hounds – no pure otterhounds, chiefly Welsh hounds and English Foxhounds. The terriers run with hounds and are topping, hardy little devils."

By 1933 Daphne was reporting on the sport with the Hawkstone for *Horse and Hound* under the pseudonym of "Heu-Gaze!" being synonymous with "Tally-Ho!" under which name she reported the doings of the Croome Foxhounds in winter. By now Arthur Jones had relinquished the Mastership to Lord Coventry, who had inherited the title and estate from his grandfather and moved both the Hawkstone

Wye Valley Otterhounds explore a likely spot around tree roots on the Windrush in 1931.

Otterhounds and his foxhounds to Croome Court. The otterhounds he took over were somewhat of a mixed bunch, including Airman, the Airedale-Foxhound cross, and Smuggler, a black Labrador-Foxhound cross, as well as several rough-coated mottled Neuadd-fawr, which were amazing hounds with fox or otter. Lord Coventry used to hunt most of his Carmarthen-bred foxhounds with the Hawkstone in the summer months, which adapted well to the new quarry. The Wye Valley had hunted draft foxhounds, with a few harriers. Daphne has said that she *"personally never liked the pure otterhound for working qualities, though his appearance is magnificent; to my mind a foxhound is infinitely quicker, less inclined to dwell, and I think, possesses a stronger constitution."*

In the early days, having relied largely on public transport to go otterhunting, Daphne now usually bicycled the nine or ten miles to Croome Court and then going on in the hound van or by car with the Master, George Coventry. This enabled her to reach the more distant meets on the Usk and the Wye and other Welsh rivers, some being as far as eighty miles away. These were long days, often three times a week, leaving home by

51

bicycle at dawn, driving several hours, walking up to fifteen miles over rough ground with the hounds and returning home by bicycle in the dark.

In April of 1933, on Easter Monday, although the meet was not far from Worcester, Daphne recalls a particularly hard day in the diary:

"A simply superb day with a most excellent hunt which everyone enjoyed enormously and a thoroughly deserved kill. There was a good crowd of holiday makers at the meet – which I reached by train, bus and, after walking some distance, a lift in the Wyatt's

The Hawkstone setting off over Leintwardine bridge to draw the river Teme, Shropshire, with Pip Stanier hunting hounds.

Vanning the Hawkstone hounds at Kinsham. Lord Coventry is facing the camera.

car. Before hounds arrived, Devereux, the water-bailiff and a keen otterhunter, took Mr Wyatt and myself down to the river to see some tracks under the bridge. They looked fairly fresh to me, but I'm not a very good judge."

The morning drag up the River Teme, a wide, deep, cold river at this time of year, eventually petered out and the Master decided to van the hounds on to the Salwarpe Brook.

"A large crowd of toughs and small children had followed to this point and we thus got rid of the majority; the really keen ones walked, and crossed by the ferry. I was breaking in a new pair of shoes today and they were just beginning to rub my heel rather unpleasantly, but I didn't want to conk out so early in the day. Hounds started drawing upstream and immediately hit off a fresh drag and there were many new tracks in the deep mud above the bridge. It was so near the Severn though, that a great many

both in pursuit of fox and otter, and his name survives in the pedigrees of hounds in well-known foxhound kennels today.]

"I thought that scent was going to improve now, as the sun had come out and warmed the water and for a very short while it did seem to be a bit better, but the improvement did not last for long and soon hounds were working on practically no scent at all.

After a period of slow and patient hunting, when it seemed as though hounds would be defeated after all, two of the old "trusties", Nailer and the half-bred Airedale, Airman, located him in a hollow tree trunk and the rest of the pack soon killed him under the bank. He was weighed out and proved to be a 21lb dog and the hunt lasted 5¼ hours finding at 2.05pm and killing at 7.20pm.

I was beginning to get a little anxious about getting home now, as the last bus goes from Worcester at 8.10pm and the last train even earlier. After a lift in the hound van, we reached Kempsey at about 9pm and they dropped me a little further on, at the Croome turn.

Harry was very concerned about me, and as a matter of fact, I began to get wind-up a bit, as I didn't care to hail a car on Bank Holiday night and we had just passed a drunk on the way and I didn't know how many more I was going to meet. I hadn't even the protection of my pole, which I had

pessimists said 'Oh, he is sure to be down in the river!' but, drawing on up, it grew a good deal fresher. The drag continued, albeit somewhat intermittently, upstream beyond the Hadley Brook junction… when suddenly they found. The otter was viewed as he set off downstream. Scent was never good and the water was as cold as it can be in mid-April. Having made an excursion up the muddy Hadley Brook, where they hunted up and down for a good half hour, they returned to the main stream.

After a while the otter landed, crossing the road by the bridge with hounds not far behind. He took to the stream below the bridge and landed on the opposite bank, continuing over the field beyond, returning to the stream before any of the hounds except Verdict had spotted him." [Croome Verdict '32 was to prove outstanding,

Followers of the Wye Valley gather on the banks of the Windrush to watch Ray Williams (far left) hunting hounds.

left in the van for Wednesday! Harry had told me it was about a mile to Severn Stoke, but it was more like 2. It was very dark and I was beginning to get rather tired, and when I reached the Gressons' gate, decided to phone from there and get brother John to fetch me in the car.

The butler had a bit of a shock at the tramp-like apparition on the front doorstep, but asked me in and I found that Mr and Mrs Gresson were still at dinner.

They were perfectly sweet to me and regaled me with soup and port (the latter, on an empty tummy, made me feel slightly tight!) and allowed me to ring up. I found that John had gone to Gloucester, so had to get Gyngell to bring a car out from the garage, which cost me 8 shillings, but I wouldn't have missed the hunt for that – it was well worth it!

We walked about 4 miles before lunch and about 4 after, so this, combined with my trek to Severn Stoke, made up a good 10 miles. I was home by about 10.30, and went straight to bed."

Lord Coventry and his wife Donne at a meet of the Croome during his Mastership.

Later that season on Derby Day, the Hawkstone met at Moreton-on-Lugg and was memorable, not only for a great hunt, but also for the fact that this was the day that Daphne met Harry Glynn, with whom she clearly fell in love.

"I went to this morning's meet with the Master and John (Coventry) from Croome in the Chrysler, which has been decarbonised and is now going like a bird. We found quite a large field waiting on the bridge, including to my surprise, Mr Addams-Williams and Ray (Ray Thompson, long-standing Master and huntsman of the Wye Valley). There was also a Border Counties member – a very tall boy called Harry Glynn – a pal of Pip's; a man from the Bucks; and Captain Williams of the Yorkshire Otterhounds. So there was a grand array of uniforms.

Hounds drew upstream for about 100 yards to a favourite holt where otters have been known to lie up, but it had been washed away during the winter, so they returned to the bridge to draw down. I started walking with Ray, who told me about a grand hunt the Wye Valley had yesterday, on this river, from Mordiford. They killed a big dog otter of 25lbs.

There was a slight touch above the station, but after this for about ¾ of a mile they were unable to own it at all until they suddenly marked their otter in a rabbit hole in the left bank at 10.40. A wonderful hunt followed, hounds working amazingly in deep and difficult water. As is so often the case with dog otters, he made downstream most of the time, with a few brief excursions upstream. I don't know who viewed him first, but I am ashamed to say it was a long time before I saw him.

He took us right down to Wergin's Bridge, below which a stickle was formed, but he slipped by Ray in the swift current and continued downstream. Our otter was getting distinctly beat after 2½ hours, and was coming up frequently to vent. He showed his muzzle above water for minutes on end and was constantly showing a chain.

As it was, we had been hunting for 3½ hours and covered a distance of about 3 miles downstream when they caught him. We nearly lost him even now, as, in getting him

Harry Glynn, 'the very epitome of life and gaiety', and almost certainly the love of Daphne's life, who was killed in action early in the war.

off hounds, he was swept away downstream by the current, with Pip gallantly hanging on and getting carried along with him! I thought we were going to lose our Secretary, but his feet touched the bottom eventually, and he waded ashore with the otter intact – a 26lb dog. It is unusual to find two dog otters in such close proximity.

I saw the Master coming in my direction with the mask and imagined he was going to give it to someone standing behind me, so that I was absolutely thrilled when he presented it to me. It's the first mask I have had and it's doubly precious after a great hunt like this. I found that Harry Glynn is a fellow reporter – he writes for the Border

Counties when he is at home, which isn't very often, as he is in the Navy."

After listening to the Derby, won that year by the legendary Hyperion, Daphne notes in her diary:

"Pip is hunting hounds to-morrow near Craven Arms, on the Onny, as three otters have been reported there and will be shot if not hunted. I asked for a lift in the van and aim to meet it at Worcester Cross at 8.30. I foresee a spot of bother at home, as the Mater doesn't like me doing two days running, but I expect I shall be able to smooth it over before I go!"

While Daphne had been given the mask of this otter, Harry Glynn was given the pole (the tail).

In the early years of the war, Harry was killed at Narvik and this pole and his hunting diaries were sent to Daphne by his sister. They were labelled and addressed in his own hand and, as Daphne says:

"I think he always had a conviction that he would not survive the war, though he was the very epitome of life and gaiety."

She describes him as "long and lean as a lamp-post, all six foot seven of him, and every inch a sportsman."

In the winter he whipped-in to several beagle packs where "his long legs enabled him to run like a lamplighter." She continued: "He possessed a sort of sophisticated school-boy humour which was very endearing; and would write scurrilous verses on otterhunting acquaintances which he sang in a charming baritone, as might be expected, with his Welsh ancestry."

Amongst Daphne's diaries is a little book containing the "Otterhunting yearbooks" from 1926 to 1938. On the cover is stuck a note, written by Daphne in a rather shaky elderly hand:

"Bequeathed to me by dear Harry Glynn. When war broke out he joined the submarines – and I never saw him again – almost inevitable."

CHAPTER SIX

Further Otterhunting Memories

It was not unusual in the autumn for Daphne to manage a morning's cubhunting before joining the otterhounds. On one such day in 1934 she left home well before 6.0am and bicycled the ten miles to the meet of the Croome at Clifton Arles.

Lord Coventry was hunting hounds and, after a somewhat scentless morning, Daphne went back to Croome to have breakfast and change into otterhunting clothes. The Hawkstone, of which Lord Coventry

was also Master of course, had met on the River Clun, and Pip Stanier, the Hunt Secretary, was hunting hounds until the Master could get there. Hounds put down their otter at the exact moment that Lord Coventry and Daphne arrived.

"Pip handed over his position as huntsman and George carried on, finally killing his otter at 4.15 after 2¾ hours hunting. I'm sure it was quite unique for an otter to be found by the Secretary and killed by the Master! It was after 7.30 when we reached

Croome so that I wasn't home till nearly 9.0 and practically dropped asleep on my bicycle."

On the last day of that season, from Ivington Bridge on the River Arrow, the Hawkstone killed their final otter of the season and Daphne returned to Croome in the hound van.

"It was 8.15 when we reached Croome and I had to ride home, precariously carrying my otter pole, in the dark, with a rather

flickering lamp, so that I was glad when I reached Tewkesbury. I do hate the end of the otterhunting season. I have hunted 73 days this season – 60 with the Hawkstone, 8 with the Wye Valley, 3 with the P.C.O.H. and 2 with the Border Counties."

In May 1938 the Hawkstone visited north Shropshire for a week.

"I made up my mind yesterday that, by fair means or foul, I would get out with the Hawkstone today. It was bound to be an

The Hawkstone returning to the Wye from Captain Hope's fishponds in 1936 with 1st whipper-in Bill Porter leading, Lord Coventry in the middle and Daphne bringing up the rear.

Daphne with fellow otter hunters at Cothi Bridge, 1937.

expensive trip and I couldn't really afford it, but I managed to make 7/6d on a few bits of jewellery which I sold in Cheltenham yesterday, which nearly paid for a car to take me in to Worcester to catch the 7.0 train. David met me at Willington, and so on to the meet at Little Bolas, arriving there before anybody at all but old Gillson and the North Shropshire huntsman.

By 10.30 there was quite a big field and, according to all accounts, I haven't missed very much for their first three days. Moving off up the Tern, hounds marked their first otter within a few fields of the meet in the same holt where they found two or three seasons ago, beneath some alders on the left bank. Two bushes lie a yard or so apart, the bank underneath being hollow for some considerable distance. In one of these,

Daphne, second from left, aged 26, with her otterhunting pole, at a meet at the Boat Inn, Whitney. One wonders how those smart leather shoes survived long days in and out of the water.

Chaplain winded the otter, which slipped down the cavity behind the bank to the other bank, where Draftsman opened at her.

Five minutes later she was viewed by Bill below. The river here is muddy and deep in places with, however, very little holding. Despite this fact the otter kept out of view altogether for the greater part of an hour, though hounds continually worked her up-stream, and down, marking her first under a hollow bank, then in a root some fifty yards below, then back up-stream to her original holt.

At length she began a long swim right up beyond this, and hounds hunted her at a tremendous pace for the next 15 minutes, driving her farther and farther up-stream and forcing her to land on more than one occasion. At exactly mid-day they turned with her down to a shallow, and closed in on her there at the end of a 70 min hunt."

A further hunt resulted in catching a veteran dog otter of 21 lbs.

"During the morning I had two invitations to stay the weekend, I felt obliged to refuse both, though I was very tempted, a) because my mother would be alone as John is away, and b) because Harry Glynn is coming to stay on Monday and goodness knows what time I should get a train home after hunting that day. However, I discovered that hounds were returning to Croome that night and Bill offered for me to come back with them. So I was over-ruled and accepted the invitation to Aqualate and this evening 'phoned home and arranged for Aunt Molly to stay to-night. Aqualate is a lovely place and the Mere is magnificent. Pip was there a few Sundays ago and came away full of enthusiasm, convinced that there were at least <u>thirty</u> otters there. He said that he could actually <u>smell</u> them, there were so many! Anyhow he's fixed a meet on the Meese, just below, on Monday, and the keeper is going to stink out the Mere in the hope that it will drive some of the numerous otters down to the river."

Daphne, centre, at Monaughty on Lugg. Kennel-huntsman and 1st whipper, Bill Porter, in foreground.

63

Daphne stayed at Aqualate Hall, a lovely house with a magnificent lake, two miles across.

"I had to live in my otterhunting change, as I had no other clothes with me, though Peggy Morris lent me evening clothes, which were too small for me! And now it is Sunday morning, and summer has come at last. As I write, the lovely Mere of Aqualate is stretched out before me like some giant's mirror, reflecting a sky of Grecian blue. What a paradise for otters!"*

However, Pip Stanier's optimism was not realised. *"We never found until just as we were finishing today and so were very late getting home, for we had quite 60 miles to go. It was 3.30, when in the last half mile of their draw, they unexpectedly put down their otter without any preliminary drag. Draftsman found her, lying rough in a*

Daphne Moore whipping-in. 1937.

big reed bed, from which they drove her with a crash into the water above the mill, to be viewed by Bill a few minutes later. There was deep water for a considerable distance – deep, muddy, and scentless. These were all the ingredients of a long, sticky hunt, despite which hounds succeeded in keeping her fairly well on the move. Certainly she took full advantage of all the many holts and hides afforded her, going from one to another and being viewed but seldom. And so the hunt went on, until at last, at 5.30, the "who-oop!" sounded after two hours hunting, and hounds broke up their fourth North Shropshire otter."

Having not reached home until after 10pm that night, it was probably fortunate that Harry Glynn, who had been hunting with the Eastern Counties that day, had telephoned to say that he would not be coming until the next morning. Harry and Daphne then went otterhunting five days in succession. *"Harry reached Gloucester about midnight last night having had a good day with the Eastern Counties and came away with the pole of the otter which they killed. He arrived here this morning at about 10.0 and we started off for the meet of the Wye Valley, which was close by at Old*

A young Ronnie Wallace whipping-in to the Wye Valley Otterhounds.

The Wye Valley on a trip to Somerset in 1937, crossing the river Brue at Alford.

Pike House. We dumped our lunch with Mathews in the hound van and went to look at hounds, who were in the field beside the Northway lane. Ron seems to have become their permanent whipper-in now and was at it again today. (After the war, as Captain Ronnie Wallace, he became one of the most influential Masters and huntsman of foxhounds of the 20th century.)

"Harry wears uniform now – Border Counties of course – and looks awfully nice in it and I think taller than ever. He's 6 foot 7 and must be finding our home very small I'm afraid."

Sadly this was a blank day, but the following day Daphne and Harry set off on bicycles for Croome where they had been offered a lift in the hound van to the meet of the Hawkstone.

"Harry and I set off soon after 8.0 this morning to the kennels. He hasn't a car of his own so we had to bicycle and the lady's bicycle which we had borrowed for him had a flat tyre before we even reached the town. So we called at the Tewkesbury Garage and hired one which was more his size. We had another contretemps before we reached Croome. I was carrying my pole and this somehow caught in the front wheel of my bicycle with the result that I went for six — but fortunately no damage was done, but for the fact that my handlebars were now pointing west instead of north, but Harry soon rectified that.

When we were on our way home from north Shropshire, we had been stopped by a policeman who told us that we were transgressing the law by having Jim (the whipper-in) on the right of the driver. As the van is built that way there doesn't seem any remedy. But now only three can go below and Harry and I therefore ascended to the roof, which we found decidedly draughty this morning. Eventually we were reduced to sitting on the floor of the well in the roof, which although rather hard and uncomfortable, was at least fairly sheltered. We were invisible from below and Pip thought we hadn't come until we arose, like Venus from the foam, and thankfully

Daphne at a mid-day break while otterhunting, a sport disparagingly described by some foxhunters as 'love and lunch'.

climbed down to comparative warmth. Even then I couldn't stop my teeth chattering for ages."

After another disappointing day when it rained heavily, it was the turn of the Wye Valley again, who met at Hampton Bridge, Evesham. *"Harry's uniform was still so wet this morning that he had to wear mufti today. And I was late and we very nearly missed the bus. We just caught it thanks to Harry's fleetness of foot, and arrived at the meet in very good time."*

After a long draw, *"a few fields below Wormington, old Dormant spoke and I suppose put off an otter lying rough. He took to water going downstream and I had a glorious view of him as his whole back, arched like a bow, showed above water at one of the shallows, below which lay a pool some seven feet deep where he chose to lie for a while. Eventually he left it to go on downstream before returning to a protective tree stump, where we thought we should have to leave him. But surprisingly enough*

Followers waiting for hounds on the drive of Croome Court at the Opening Meet of the Hawkstone in 1936. Daphne third from left.

he didn't linger there and we had quite a lively little hunt now until they caught him in deep water where Ron dived in and grabbed the corpse and brought our otter to shore after 2 hours of tricky hunting. He weighed 22lbs."

The following day, also with the Wye Valley, Daphne did not hunt as it was the Croome Puppy show. *"I only went to the meet this morning as the Puppy Show started at 11.30, but I decided to go on the bus with Harry and see them start, and then Collie was going to pick me up on the corner and convey me to the kennels. Nobody at the meet recognised me in my best clothes and they wondered who on earth Harry had picked up! At about 5.30 Harry returned, soaked to the skin, with the mask. They had quite a fair hunt and I wish I'd been there."*

The last of the five consecutive days was with the Hawkstone again. *"This morning Harry and I armed ourselves well with rugs and coats and groundsheets and made ourselves a warm and comfortable eyrie on the top of the van. I wish I could report a rousing hunt but to tell the truth we experienced one of the dullest and slowest which I have ever known. The eventual hunt lasted for 3 hours 20 minutes and heaven preserve me from another like it! It was awfully disappointing that Harry saw such poor sport with the Hawkstone. It's always the way, when one wants hounds to excel."*

Harry then departed northwards and Daphne climbed back on the hound van to travel south. The end of what must have been a blissful week for Daphne with the man she clearly adored.

Daphne had owned, from her early days of otterhunting, a greatly treasured, ash otter pole. These poles were an important part of an otterhunter's equipment to help them crossing the

Part of the Will written for Daphne by her Hawkstone friends at the Porth Hotel.

country and, in particular, to help keep their balance when crossing the river. She had always joked that she wished to be buried with her pole in order to be able to cross the River Styx into the afterlife. Unusually for an otterhunter, Daphne was a non-swimmer.

One night, after dinner, when staying at the Llandysul pub with the rest of the Hawkstone party, it was decided that she should make a last Will and Testament. A legal and binding document was drawn up, with George Coventry and Pip Stanier named as her executors. Various bequests of a hunting nature were made and a clause added: "I desire on my death that my otterhunting pole shall be placed in my coffin and buried with me."

"All was duly signed and witnessed – and then, to my horror, that prize idiot Copner actually went and posted the thing! He addressed it, with a covering letter enclosed, to Lloyds Bank, where I shall never dare to show my face again."

It was some weeks later when she finally summoned up the courage to call at the bank and pay the sum of 2s 6d to retrieve it from the strong room. The original document is in her diary of that year and, as she says, *"it would have proved a great embarrassment to my survivors had it remained as my final Will,*

since the pole measured between six and seven feet in length!"

George Coventry had a great sense of humour, which is evident in a letter amongst Daphne's papers, written by George to the Hawkstone Secretary, Pip Stanier, on Croome Court paper on 28th September 1937, after a season when he had been unable to hunt hounds himself due to a duodenal ulcer:

My Dear Pip,
Thank you for hunting my hounds for me all this season. I think you have done very well to kill 42 otters. At the moment I hate all females except my wife. First a girl staying here tried to get off with me, Donne (his wife) was amused, but she was rather pretty and I was not. Then Princess Marie Louise seems to be staying indefinitely with my mother.
I like her, but she disapproves of me and expects me to shock her. I have done so religiously up to date, but it's difficult to keep up. Then we found a badger and some blasted girl thought she'd come and help the hounds kill it, and did

At the door of the Porth Hotel on the river Ceri, the scene of the writing of Daphne's 'mock will'. Daphne linking arms with Pip Stanier and Captain Eden Wallace, Ronnie's father, far right.

everything wrong she could, so that I got bitten (that's why I didn't come out on Saturday). Then Daphne had a young man out yesterday, whom she wanted to show off to, and became so much the Master that she even told me how to look after my hounds, and I'm afraid that I told her off rather severely.

We had a nice hunt yesterday and killed our fox in the open in style. It's so much more satisfactory than the "was finally accounted for", but I've never

sweated so much in all my life. It was a very hot day and we couldn't find foxes early, it was 10.30 before we found and then scent was bad in covert, so I let them run. Hunting kit is made for winter and hounds were going so fast that we had to gallop all out to keep with them at all. They've got a grand cry this year.

I don't yet know the puppies' notes individually, but I'm not losing the music and I think it's improving. I've had hounds for 17 years now and in about

another 10 years I ought to have a pack that really suits me, and by then I'll probably be too slow to keep with them, so it will be all done to no purpose.

> Yours ever,
> George

PS. I certainly shall be too slow as I'm getting them faster every year and I can't get near them on a good scent now.

However, during the 1938 season, with war looming, George Coventry resigned his mastership of the Hawkstone Otterhounds. At a General Meeting of the hunt in September it was agreed that Captain Eden Wallace, Ronnie's father, and Pip Stanier should take over as Joint Masters. *Out hunting the previous day, Daphne writes: "Today was one of the most dismal, dreadful days I have ever known. War-clouds have been gathering for weeks now and war seems inevitable – so I started feeling in the depths of gloom, which the newspaper I bought on route did nothing to dispel."*

At the end of the day she continues:

"Not a cheerful day at all. And tomorrow is the Members' meeting at Ludlow, which will be a depressing affair too."

After a morning's cubhunting at Croome in October, Daphne walks out with Bill and the otterhounds. *"After today I feel that I can bear the thought of hounds leaving Croome even less than before. And Bill is going – so that will be another link broken. I am determined to see as much of them as I can before they depart to their new kennels at the Wallaces new house near Ludlow."*

A testimonial was organised for the outgoing Master and a painting of Donne, his wife, was presented to them at the 1939 Opening Meet, by which time George Coventry had joined the Army. He wrote to Daphne:

> My Dear Daphne,
> Thank you so much for sending me on the H.O.H. letters. They were very nice, and it was very nice indeed of you to have taken all the trouble you have over the presentation. I hope to get out

Lord Coventry (foreground) at a meet of the Croome in the village of Fladbury.

next week, but at present I am very busy being a soldier at Norton Barracks. It is most interesting — I can take a Brenn Gun down into about 30 different pieces, and then watch someone else try to put it together again!

Yours ever

George

In April 1939 Daphne writes: "*Otterhunting has started again and already the Hawkstone have had two early bye-days. To my everlasting sorrow I could not be with them, for there is now no kindly hound-van to "lift" me from Croome, and though I have bought an Austin Seven for £12, I failed in my first driving test, and anyhow doubt whether it will ever survive the long journeys to Wales. I suppose that I shall have to have another shot at getting my licence, but I detest driving and nothing but otterhunting would ever make me attempt it. Hounds left Croome at the New Year and I hated them going. No more walking out with hounds, watching them feed, seeing*

Charles Parker and Ronnie Wallace (both sitting) at lunch, discussing the day so far with members of the field, overlooking the Wye.

them in kennel, travelling with them on the van. Captain Wallace has made a clean sweep as regards the Hunt Staff. Stallard (from the Courtenay Tracey) has come as 1st whip and K. H, and Charlie Bundy's son, Henry, is 2nd whip. He is very young, only 15, but he has been more or less brought up with hounds and seems to know his job."

This last summer before war was declared provided some wonderful otterhunting and it soon became apparent that in the young Ronnie Wallace, who was now hunting hounds jointly with Pip Stanier, there was a quite exceptional talent. Little more than two months before the outbreak of war the Hawkstone had a day which many experienced otterhunters said was the best day they had ever experienced. It was the first day of a Joint Week with the Wye Valley and hounds met on the ancient ten-arched bridge at Crickhowell.

"There was an immense field – I have never, I think, seen a larger. People from at least six hunts were represented. Hounds

marked their first otter within 500 yards of the bridge and there followed a fascinating hunt of three hours before accounting for a 22lb dog otter."

Writing her report for *Horse and Hound*, Daphne states:

"There is so much to write of the hunting from Crickhowell on June 26ᵗʰ that all the ink in south Wales would be exhausted before I could tell the story in full." But her report of the second hunt continues: *"Everyone was well satisfied after this, but still better was to come. After lunch we reached Glanusk, and there a second otter awaited us in the old holt above the bridge. The otter bolted, and we could see his every movement in the gin-clear water as he turned up-stream, almost every whisker visible to us on the steep, grassy bank above.*

Then came the pack, hunting with a cry which defies description. Tasty led them up the pool, throwing her tongue all the way, over the ford and still up-stream, with the rest pressing on behind in a quickly swelling chorus. Above lay the grotto, where rough water foams about the rocks and the current is very strong.

On reaching this, hounds came at last to a check, and were cast back, marking their otter in a culvert in the wood above the rocks. The terrier soon had him away, and he made a spectacular exit as he dived through mid-air down the steep bank to

the water. For a while now he kept to the rocky stretch below the island itself. Then he crossed to the covert on the right bank, and hounds were coursing him as he galloped overland, the leading hounds rolling him over as he reached the water again. He then slipped across the island, down the stretch on the far side, and was viewed below before he came back over the island, with the pack in full cry close behind. On regaining the water, they checked, and it was thanks to Valentine that they killed him, for he was most probably making for the canal. Evidently he landed unseen in the covert at the same point as before, and Valentine took the line, speaking all the way, up the bank for a considerable distance.

The others joined him and overhauled their otter on the slope, the whole pack rolling down with him on to the shingle below. He proved to be very old, and weighed no less than 26lbs. Time 65 minutes. So ended one of the finest hunts it is possible to see."

The last day before the outbreak of war was from the Radnorshire Arms, Presteigne and Daphne's diary starts with the quote *"All joy is darkened and the mirth of the land is gone."*

"Today was unpleasantly reminiscent of the zero day of the September crisis, and I never wish to spend another like it. Probably we shall never see hounds again —

if war comes Captain Wallace hopes to keep three couple for as long as possible, as the nucleus of a new pack should hunting ever start again. But even that seems doubtful. It was a miserable day, the weather seeming in tune with our own mood of gloom and apprehension.

At the end of the unsuccessful day, Pip took me to the Radnorshire Arms, where we changed, and wanted me to stay for a drink. He said it would probably be our last together. But I hadn't the heart to stay and instead fled to my car and came unhappily home.

I wonder if this is the last day's hunting I shall have – I think probably so. Nothing would give me a greater pleasure than to see that man Hitler put in the boiler and fed to hounds. Only perhaps it wouldn't be fair to hounds…"

Daphne's pre-war diary concludes: "*On September 1st, in the early hours of the morning, Germany started her attack on Poland. At 11.o'c on Sunday, the 3rd, we formally declared War, and at 5.o'c that afternoon France joined with us against Germany in what will inevitably be the greatest and most calamitous conflict of all time.*

No one can foresee the end of it and probably, by the time it is over, there will not be much left to live for. Hunting will almost certainly die a natural death and whether or not a certain amount of hounds may be kept on to preserve the breed remains to be seen. At all events, I doubt if our generation will see otterhunting again."

CHAPTER SEVEN

The War Years

In July 1939, at the last Peterborough Royal Foxhound Show before the outbreak of war, an unentered doghound, Croome Sailor, won the first class. He was not of the heavier orthodox type usually seen at Peterborough at that time and this was a triumph for his breeder, Lord Coventry, who passionately believed in the more active Welsh-cross type of hound.

A report of that show notes: *"In Class 1 the first prize went to Croome Sailor, a very smart young dog with conspicuous tick markings on a white forehand. What was more conspicuous was his beautiful liberty of action. Sailor has not too much bone; in fact he is rather light of bone, but was it not Lord Henry Bentick himself who spoke of bone as "that useless encumbrance?" "*

George Coventry wrote to Daphne following the show:

My Dear Daphne,
Thank you so much for your words. Sailor won fairly comfortably. Cardinal was kept in till the last four, but I don't like him, although he didn't look bad with the others. All the other entries were most orthodox, except the South and West Wilts, which were nice. I think and hope that Sailor thoroughly shocked all the Old Brigade."
Yours ever, George

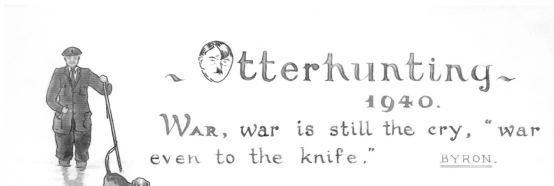

War was declared two months later and the world that Daphne knew fell apart. A year on and both her mentor and father-figure, George Coventry, and the man she undoubtedly loved, Harry Glynn, were both dead, killed in action.

Given his age in 1939, which was 38, Lord Coventry's application to join the Army was turned down. He complained to the King, who knew him, and the King intervened to allow him to enlist. Lieut, the Earl of Coventry then joined 7th Battalion, the Worcester Regiment, who embarked in January 1940 for Le Havre and moved up towards Brussels. However, they were then caught up in May that year in the German advance that led to the British evacuation from Dunkirk.

The Worcesters held up the Germans for four vital days, but in doing so could not reach Dunkirk before the last ships departed for England. Lord Coventry's unit were amongst those left to their fate. It was reported in England that the Earl of Coventry was officially missing, presumed dead. It was relatively recently that his daughter, Lady Maria Coventry, met the priest who had buried him and lived long enough to be able to tell her the terrible truth of his death.

The SS Panzer Commander contacted this priest in Givenchy-les-la-Bassée near Lille to say that if the remaining British force that had held them up were to surrender, he would not destroy the village. In the event though, he took revenge for the casualties inflicted on his unit and had the disarmed Lord Coventry shot while on his knees in the village square.

The priest buried him, along with eighteen others and was able to tell Lady Maria, many years later, of the nature of his murder.

This SS Panzer Division, which also provided guards for the concentration camps, committed a number of atrocities in the area on this same day, including the massacre of a hundred disarmed British prisoners of war not far away in Le Paradis.

Harry Glynn had written to Daphne from *HMS Kimberley*, sending her his hunting diaries:

Dear Daff,

The time has come to evacuate my Hunting Diaries – here they are for safe-keeping – read them if you wish. I'll write properly soon – great haste at the moment.

Good hunting,
Harry

He never did write, but his death appeared in the papers: GLYNN – killed on active service – Lieut Henry Trelawnay Dashper Glynn R.N, son of the late Mr & Mrs J. B. Glynn of Neston and brother of Mrs M. C. Wainwright of Northfield House, Stamford.

Hounds were put down in great numbers as hunts either disbanded completely or managed to keep going with a few hounds, a skeleton staff, mostly elderly or very young, and elderly or lady Masters.

Daphne Moore, at about the time that she was hunting regularly with Harry Glynn.

Daphne wrote a poem, published in *Horse and Hound*, in which she lamented the death of so many hounds:

THE MURDER OF THE INNOCENTS

Empty kennels! The very words are haunted
By the sad ghosts of hounds so lately dead;
Murdered by reason of a War unwanted,
Mourned with a heavy heart and tears unshed.

Empty kennels! No hound-song greets our waking,
No clamour sounds the knell of passing day.
A deathly silence reigns when dawn is breaking;
Quiet, when the sun goes on its westerly way.

Empty kennels! The very stones are crying
To add their voices to our sad laments
For well-loved hounds, who suffered by their dying,
A second Murder of the Innocents.

Pip Stanier's wartime letter to Daphne saying that hounds were to be put down.

In 1940 Daphne wrote:

"Since last season ended I went to Clifton Court to work on the farm there, and very pleasant it was, though in the haymaking it was pretty stiff and some nights I was so tired that I hardly knew how to walk to the house! However, I soon got used to it and enjoyed life there as well as it is possible to do in War-time. I planned to stay here until such a time as I should be required by the Army Remount Depot, to which I had *applied for a job. But — the best laid plans of mice and men, etc — on Monday morning two weeks ago Nemesis overtook me.*

That fool Major, the heavy-weight hunter, took it into his wooden head to bolt with me on the horse-rake (after six hours of it in the clover field!) and I fell beneath the wheel, which well flattened me. The muscles of my right leg were squashed considerably and I have been laid up completely until the end of this week."

"The best laid plans"… as I said before — and instead of being at Melton Mowbray this week on the Remounts job, as I expected, here I am at the Croome kennels, my Mecca which I never thought to attain.

A page from one of Daphne's diaries shows the meticulous care she must have taken to create this cut-out montage.

It happened like this…

I was to have gone up to Melton on Saturday, by which time the doctor guaranteed that I should be capable of working, though my leg will never be really sound for some while. In the meantime, however, I was offered the job of helping Reg Blizard in the Croome kennels, for Pavitt, alas! has gone as huntsman to the North Warwickshire and Joe has been called up.

After much deliberation, therefore, I decided to come to Croome – as I had always wished to do and as I had hoped to do under George's Mastership upon Joe going into the Army. That hope is now gone forever, and things at Croome can never, never be the same; but I do feel that George would have liked his hounds to be kept going, and he wrote to me last season that he was all for keeping everything going as nearly as if there were no War as possible.

The Hawkstone hounds on the River Clettwr in 1940.

I am thankful that the committee has decided to keep the pack at Croome instead of sending them to the Ledbury kennels as originally intended. That would have been fatal, for I am sure that hounds would never have been seen at Croome again. As it is, only 11½ couple have been kept, 4½ of which are entered. The oldest hounds in kennel are three season hounds and most of my friends have gone. It is not the least of Hitler's atrocities."

However, having registered the previous December, Daphne took up the job as a groom at the Army Remounts Depot at Melton Mowbray, but had to return after a few months to nurse her mother who had become ill. One can't help wondering if this was a ploy to get her daughter home. Her car having finally broken, she found a farm job within bicycling distance of Tewkesbury. *"I miss my hounds and my kennel life, bitterly, and suppose that I shall always do so. My heart, whatever my work may be – will always be at Croome…"*

Following the death of Lord Coventry, Lieut. J. Shirley Priest was appointed Master & Huntsman. However, you will not find his name in the list of former Masters of the Croome listed in *Baily's Hunting Directory*. This is because he was forced to resign in disgrace. Daphne takes up the story:

"I had heard a rumour that Shirley, who until now has flourished like the Green Bay Tree, has been apprehended in his crimes and that he is languishing under close arrest at the moment. The charge brought against him is that of using Army petrol and personnel for his own purposes, and I am thankful that I am not at kennels to be questioned, for the hunt is bound to be involved. Syd was undeniably kennel staff and scarcely saw the Barracks except on Pay Day, and some of those Army vehicles were almost daily in use as flesh carts.

Besides all this he had grooms and a keeper conscripted for his benefit, and apparently his private cars have been run on Army petrol. Reg was at first almost completely mute on the subject; later he confirmed most of the rumours and admitted being questioned by the police. Syd, naturally, has been removed."

Lieut. J. S. Priest was found guilty of 12 charges and was sentenced to be cashiered and imprisoned for one year.

"I am so much afraid that all this will impact on my precious hounds for certainly the Committee will now raise the cry once more of "off with their heads"! And I cannot bear the thought of them being put to death. They are all my very real friends — far more so than the majority of human friends."

In spite of still being 'winged' and now having to carry my arm in a sling [she was off work, having pulled a tendon on the farm], *I succeeded in bicycling over to Croome to see hounds this afternoon. Sad news was awaiting me; the expected slaughter has begun and I found that of the dogs only Limerick and Limber were left, and all but 9½ couple of bitches gone. It was terrible to see such a depleted pack. I went down the paddock with them and adored them more than ever. I cannot bear it if these have to go. Even Carmen and old Avril seemed overjoyed to see me, and I*

Pip Stanier, variously Hunt Secretary, Master and huntsman of the Hawkstone Otterhounds.

Life must go on: the opening meet in 1940 outside The Lion, at Leintwardine.

was smothered in mud from welcoming paws when I came away."

At the start of her 1942–43 diary, Daphne brings the hunting arrangements up to date:

"Since Shirley Priest's court-martial, the Hunt Committee more or less lay down and died. There was no Master or huntsman, no one to finance the pack, no one to take the slightest interest in the affairs of the Hunt. Hunting this season seemed out of the question, but miracles do happen and a Master suddenly came forward in the shape of Mr Langham-Miller, who hunted with us

a few days last season and was very anxious to keep the Croome alive in spite of the many handicaps. Finally, after two Committee meetings, he was appointed Joint-Master with Donne (Lord Coventry's widow) and this at his most generous suggestion, for I imagine that he supplies the necessary £.s.d. Kenneth Farr was persuaded to take on the job of hunting hounds, although he has never done so before. He knows the game and is a good horseman. Moreover, he is a farmer and this will be greatly in his favour. Altogether, I think we are very lucky and, given a chance, should be able to have sport and kill foxes this season."

The bulk of Daphne's farm job was now delivering milk seven days a week, but when offered horses by Harry Gittins, *"the thought of hunting on Saturdays was like a breath of life in the present stale existence and I made up my mind to achieve it somehow. Accordingly I approached my boss and boldly asked for Saturdays off — with a drop in wages, of course, to balance it, and my request was granted."*

However, there were not as many Saturdays off as Daphne anticipated and, with hounds, under wartime conditions, only hunting two days a week and finishing the season at the end of January, she did not get as much hunting as she would have liked and so resigned from the milk round job.

Daphne was now writing more articles, particularly for *The Field*. The Editor was Brian Vesey-Fitzgerald, operating from a temporary wartime address in Winchester, Hampshire.

While writing to her full address of "The Gastons, Tewkesbury", in October 1941, accepting an article for publication, he interestingly adds, *"I am glad to hear that your brother is back on a month's sick leave — a month does not sound very long — and I am glad that he is energetic enough to do a novel. When he has finished that and if he has enough energy when he has finished, you must just stand over him and tell him I would like a couple of articles on fishing."*

The articles she wrote, which are pasted into her diaries, include: "Peep-o'-Day Hunting: a Memory of 1940"; "Opening Meet – a Reverie"; "Tough Men of the Chase"; "Sketches behind the Scenes"; and "Thoughts on War-Time Hunting." Historical articles included "Books for the Bloodied", and "An Excursion into the Past."

Later, the Editor of *The Field* wrote: *"Thank you very much for your Christmas Card. I did not send any being far too broke. I hope that 1942 will find your finances, which appear to be worrying, going from strength to strength. To assist them, if only a little, I wonder if you like to write an article on the Government of Foxhunting in the Future? I am sure you have a few ideas on so pertinent a question."*

In June 1943 Daphne wrote,

"An interval between changing jobs has given me the chance of seeing some neighbouring kennels and I'm emulating Mr Sponge."

On the first day she hitch-hiked to Broadway and, having got a good "lorry-hop", she arrived early and had to *"cool my heels in this bogus, unedifying village for nearly an hour."* Nowadays, swarming with tourists, many people might agree with her view of some 75 years ago!

The 'magical' huntsman, George Gillson, who had whipped-in to Frank Freeman at the Pytchley and hunted the Warwickshire with such brilliance from 1935 to 1940 and 1945 to 1956.

The North Cotswold, like all other hunts operating under wartime conditions, had very few hounds in kennels and Daphne notes,

"They have, I believe, 15 couple altogether. But they have their own strains safe in America (Mr Mason Houghland of the Hillsboro' had over 20 couple shipped over to him on the outbreak of War) so can draw on that source when victory comes."

Mason Houghland is the grandfather of the present Master of the Midland Foxhounds, and former President of the MFHA of America, Mason Lampton.

"The Master, Major Scott, was on active service, but has been invalided home from the Middle East and now has a staff job at Sandhurst. He is hoping to put in a day's hunting occasionally. Hounds looked extremely well, though possibly a bit on the light side. George [George Goodwin, Major Bill Scott's kennel-huntsman, who hunted hounds in his absence] *gets pig food for his ration and they seem to do all right on it. Their coats look lovely. He gets his knackers in with a horse-drawn van; the Master's old grey hunter in the shafts! Hounds hunted three days a week throughout the season and had 73 days in all, killing a great many foxes. They really are a grand pack."*

However, Daphne was less impressed on her next kennel visit the following day, to the Ledbury.

"Saw another pack of hounds this-afternoon – the Ledbury this time – but was not favourably impressed. They are poor material at the best of times as far as looks are concerned, and now, living as they do on potatoes and flesh, they are a desperate sight. I bicycled to kennels, a very long way it seemed in the heat, arriving just after 3.0.

Hoare and old Harry Roake are still there, but Hoare is becoming very fed up and talks of leaving, though I don't suppose he really will. It was ages before I saw the hounds, who were out in the grass yard, for Hoare is such a talker that it's impossible to get him to come to a check within half an hour."

Having remarked in her diary on all the old hounds, of which there were 20 couple, Hoare brought out the three couple of young ones to be entered that autumn.

"These really were a contrast to the old hounds. They looked well, though painfully light, with a bloom on their coats, whereas the old hounds' coats were dull and staring. They had real good necks and shoulders and can gallop like the wind as they soon showed me when they were turned out in the grass yard. They all need to fill out a lot, but can't do it without proper food. Apparently Hoare doesn't get any rations at all, so it isn't his fault that they look half-starved. He hardly seemed to know that rations are due to him; there must be very bad management somewhere."

A few days later, staying with the Staniers, Daphne visited the North Shropshire.

"I have never been to the kennels there, and was surprised to find what beautiful kennels they are. Still more was I surprised by hounds themselves, which I had always thought to be heavy, lumbering, English-y types; instead of which I found a really lovely lot of bitches, some very passable dogs, and all looking in the very pink of condition. They are fed on flesh — cooked flesh, exclusively, except during a shortage in the past fortnight when they had to switch over to their rations. Johnson physics them regularly once a week and attributes their good condition to this. The kennels are very roomy and light and the lodges well-planned and well-drained.

We had a rare old kennel gossip. There is always plenty to talk about to Hunt Servants and I love the breed. It is a queer sort of brotherhood and every Hunt Servant one meets, knows, or is known by, a dozen or more mutual acquaintances."

The Worcestershire were the next pack to be visited, *"so yesterday evening I rang up Gillson* [Sam Gillson, father of the legendary Warwickshire huntsman, George Gillson] *and arranged to go over there this afternoon. I had an early lunch and left about 1.0 to hitch-hike. Gillson was in kennels. He is such a charming old man, one of the really old-fashioned type of Hunt Servant, and in his day was, I believe, a great huntsman. He hunted the Cottesmore for years under Lord Lonsdale and his father hunted them before him. He is most interesting to talk to and I loved hearing his reminiscences.*

The Worcestershire are very heavy, with a lot of bone – pretty good, I think, of their type, but I have been brought up to quite a different standard. Put a Worcestershire doghound beside, say, our Limerick (Croome), and the comparison would, to my mind, be odious. But of course that's only my opinion. There are 20 odd couple of hounds in kennels and 12 couple of whelps, which is pretty good in Wartime."

Having described all the hounds she saw, she was shown around the kennels.

"I saw the feed-house and boiler room, where they have an old-fashioned open copper. Gillson told me a horrific story of the North Warwickshire kennelman, who, many years ago, fell into one of his steam coppers and was literally boiled to death. This happened when Gillson himself was a whipper-in there.

He is full of old tales and most entertaining. His father, he said, well remembered the Midnight Steeplechase which (and this I didn't know) was an annual affair at Melton. He can himself recall Mr Tailby, Bay Middleton and the Empress of Austria, "Brooksby" and many more famous foxhunting people. We walked together to his house and I was on the point of departing when he said surely I was going to have some tea.

Inside I found a magnificent meal laid, all ready for me and dear old Mrs Gillson (who is the great Frank Freeman's sister) waiting for us to come in. I thoroughly enjoyed myself, for they were both so enormously interesting. Mrs Gillson was born and bred in kennels, for her father hunted the North Hereford and her two brothers, Frank and Will, are justly celebrated. I thought it was about 6 o'clock when I left and was horrified to find that it was getting on for 7.30. Mrs Gillson walked with me to the main road and I was lucky getting a lorry all the way home."

These kennel visits were the first of many and were developed in 1951 into a popular weekly series of articles for *Horse and Hound* entitled "Round the Kennels."

CHAPTER EIGHT

The Latter War Years and the Holland-Martin Family

Daphne started the season 1943-44 working for Harry Gittins, both on the farm and with the horses. The first morning's cubhunting was typical in that Daphne was put on a horse that was one of a batch that had arrived on the boat from Ireland the previous night.

However, she was finding it increasingly difficult to work for her extremely bad-tempered employer.

"Since last Saturday there have been vast upheavals, and at last the old man's temper became so fearful and matters came to such a pitch that he ordered me to go – and I went!

It all began with a frightful ride which I had, bringing a horse from Worcester Station on Thursday night. He was as nappy as they're made and reared and napped it all the way from Shrub Hill to Clifton so that I was pretty shaken by the time I reached the farm. I only had a blasting from the old

Thurston and Ruby Holland-Martin by the gates at Overbury Court.

man for giving the horse a thrashing which he thoroughly deserved. The next morning was worse, terminating in a battle royal and my departure. But I am very sad indeed at leaving, for I love the farm and love the work and love the horses — though I hate and fear the owner."

By the Opening Meet in 1944 Daphne writes:

"Since last season I have seen very, very little of hounds and have – for the first time for about fifteen years and more – had no cubhunting. But I have a glorious job and have nothing to complain about, for since March I have been working at the Overbury Stud – the Holland-Martins – and adore it there."

Tim Holland-Martin well remembers those days, when, as a boy of about ten, Daphne taught him to ride. His father, Cyril, was one of six brothers who were brought up on the estate. Their father died towards the end of the war, but their mother, who Tim describes as a "Victorian matriarch," still organised the house; while Thurston ran the estate, the farm and the stud. Ruby and Thurston were the keenest horsemen, both hunting regularly and riding in point-to-points.

In later years the Overbury Stud became very well-known indeed, but, even in those early days, the yearling colts they sent to the sales at Newmarket were making their mark. Daphne worked as a groom for both the stud and the hunters, with special responsibility for the gundog kennels. She also filled in the pedigree books for the stud in her immaculate script.

Thurston Holland-Martin, who managed the estate and stud at Overbury.

Daphne was a particularly strong character and Mrs Holland-Martin enjoyed her 'get up and go' attitude and treated her almost as family.

Ruby Holland-Martin.

91

Thurston was also particularly good to her, encouraging her to see the dogs working out shooting, taking her racing to Cheltenham and involving her in the social life of the estate. As a small boy, Tim remembers her as a 'character', with a deep voice, talking incessantly about hounds and hunting on their rides together.

In March 1944, the war still over-shadowed everyone's lives and Daphne writes: *"The bombing of London has started again with renewed violence, and London has almost nightly raids now, comparable to the blitz of 1940. This morning I had a lift with a couple of charming Cockney lorry drivers who told me just how bad it had been. It is Mamma's birthday. Birthday presents are difficult to get now, but I bought her a 2/6d stamp book and managed to get some surplus soap and Rinso from the village shop."*

She also writes of her brother's future wife for the first time: *"John writes of a new girl-friend, Lucile by name. He sounds quite serious about her, but he is a very fickle lover."*

Daphne's interest and knowledge of pedigrees was undoubtedly developed while working for the Holland-Martins.

"I have borrowed a book on Bloodstock breeding by Miller; very interesting. I went in to work on the pedigrees and before I had been at it long two of the many Court minions appeared to lay tea – which they always have in the Billiard Room, where I work. It transpired that it was to be a tea-party and I asked if I might take my cup of tea into my corner and go on working – which I did. Thurston and Tadpole arrived around 5.0 and Thurston gave me a hand in looking up things in the General Stud Book and also produced the 1802 volume, wherein I mean to trace our mares back to Eclipse and the Arabians!"

Daphne working in the stables at Overbury Court with groom, Charlie Morris (left) and Stud Groom, Jack Nicholls.

Daphne riding one of her favourites, Whitesand, in front of the stables at Overbury Court.

Jack Nicholls was undoubtedly a top class stud groom and had run the North Cotswold Hunt stables for Bill Scott before the war. However, one gets the impression from Daphne's diaries that he may have slightly resented her special relationship with the family and took the opportunity of putting her in her place when the opportunity arose.

It was September 1945 and the war was over, although, strangely, there is little reference to the fact in her diary. Daphne was looking forward to riding her favourite, Whitesand, at Evesham Show.

"I rode darling Whitesand up bareback and he was so good. But his curby hock is up and he won't be able to go to Evesham Show. Everything was beastly to-day. Somehow I felt out of it all; Jack took the Cyril H-M. boys (Tim and his brother) for their ride, criticised my washing of Goldfinch's fetlocks, and requested that I should take his wife and Charlie in my car to-morrow, whilst the others ride. If Ruby doesn't come (he may not) Jack will show both Crumb and Hardrada – and we do feel that we might be allowed a ride each."

The day-to-day work in the stables continued with Daphne working with Stud groom, Jack Nicholls, and a good old-fashioned sort, Charlie Morris. The star of the stable was Hefty, who Thurston rode, and won the Lady Dudley Cup (the Gold Cup of the Point to Pointing world) on him. It is interesting to note that his nephew, Tim Holland-Martin, won the same race in the 1960s on a horse called Midnight Coup.

The following day she writes; *"Ruby did come after all and I quite enjoyed the show. I didn't have to take my car, which was a relief, as it would have been grossly overloaded and I do want to get to Newmarket next week."* At the end of her description of the show, she notes:

"The Heavyweight Hunter class was won by Beau Geste, ridden by Gittins. This horse later won the Championship, but unfortunately for old man Gittins, after galloping full split around the ring, he pulled up too quickly, and the horse shot him out of the saddle in a glorious voluntary! It was very undignified, but the commentator tried to make things better by saying that a dog had run out and startled the horse. There was no dog within miles!"

With her increasing interest in bloodstock, Daphne had said how much she would like to visit Newmarket for the Sales, and Mrs Holland-Martin arranged for her to stay with friends there during her week's holiday. Daphne took Anne Coventry with her, but was not impressed with the somewhat unconventional design of their billet.

Cyril Holland-Martin, one of the six Holland-Martin sons, with his own three boys, Geoffrey, Timothy and Robin.

"This is a most incredible house – a sort of converted barn. Within, all American luxury – but the walls fall down at a touch and mice gnaw through the ceilings! One reaches the front door by a flight of steep wooden stairs with a rope handrail; the kitchen and living rooms are here, the bedrooms and bathroom are on the ground-floor on the opposite side of the yard. We went to the stables to see the Arabs, with Bunty, the girl groom. There were two stallions, Harab and Charbi. I was a little disappointed in this, my first view of Arabs; they seemed coarse compared with my conception of the breed. There are mares and foals out in the fields – also Suffolk Punches.

The next day was the first day of the Sales:

"It was exciting to see 'Park Paddocks' and the Sales ring and the yearlings being paraded, and to try to spot 'personalities' – Phil Bull, the Duke and Duchess of Norfolk, Lord Willoughby de Broke. We sat in the Sales ring most of the day; it was all a novel experience for us. The bidding was swift and the auctioneers – particularly the young one – wizards of quickness, with eyes everywhere at once.

The first lot was a chestnut filly by Foxhunter out of Duce II. She fetched 2,400 gns. This was quite a good price – rather above the average, but during the day there were some very high prices reached: -

6,600 gns for a filly by Fair Trial; 6,800 gns for a Stardust colt; 9,500 gns for a Nearco colt."

Following a day's racing, Daphne set off to see some of the Studs.

"I wasn't highly successful at first in seeing the Studs. Unfortunately Thurston hasn't come to these Sales, otherwise I might have tried for some introductions." After managing to see several Studs and racing stables, she returned to the Sales. "The sale of another Nearco colt out of Rosy Legend was very dramatic. There was a hush, then an outbreak of talk as he was led in. The crowd broke the barriers and had to be forcibly restrained. Finally he was knocked down to that repulsive black man – the Maharajah Gaekwad of Baroda – for the fantastic sum of 28,000 gns. And he may never turn out any good at all."

Back at Overbury, life continued as before and hunting was beginning to find some sort of normality again. *"I rang up the Master to-night. He tells me that there is to be a Croome Hunt Ball next month. I think I'll ask Dalesman to come."*

Some fifteen years older than Daphne and certainly something of a 'likeable rogue', it is interesting that Daphne always had a soft spot for him. But her mother would definitely not have approved! On November 10th 1945 the Croome held their traditional

Ruby Holland-Martin riding in the Lady Dudley Cup at the Worcestershire point-to-point in 1938.

Opening Meet at Croome Court and Daphne rode a young horse she had brought on. *"Salient has proved himself a marvellous hunter and I feel proud of him. It was a poor day really, but quite good fun."*

She wrote the day up in the local papers under her pseudonym of "Tally-Ho", but did of course not comment on the former disgraced Master, as she did in the diary. *"Shirley was out, behaving and looking like the cad he is, rushing about madly and nearly jumping on to hounds."*

With the war over and hunting starting properly again, it seems that Daphne was feeling increasingly unsettled in her role at Overbury. The occasional remark in her diary shows this.

"I feel tired, discouraged and miserable, and I don't feel that anyone likes me." And another day, *"a beastly day again. I feel all the resentment, jealousy and misery inside boiling up within. I feel just a servant, and I wanted to go to the Croome Hunt Ball*

next week and try to forget myself a bit, but Billy Buckley, whom I asked, has just wired to say he can't make it after all, so that's that." The family of course remained very fond of Daphne and were fully supportive. The staff probably resented her unusual status. *"Jack was in a horrible socialistic mood this evening and I felt like hitting him."* Her entry after January 2nd 1946 sums up the situation.

"To-night was the Land Girls Party, given by them in the Village Hall. I stayed the night at the Court for it, but didn't enjoy myself. I was overdressed, over-tired and not in the mood for a party. Thurston did M.C. I had four horses to exercise to-day as Georgie had the afternoon off in order to cut sandwiches. Slept badly after the party — worked before breakfast, in the dog-kennels, breakfasted and lunched with the Holland-Martins."

There was a major set-back a few weeks later when Daphne suffered a bad fall on the road when an American ambulance came by her so fast and so close *"that it nearly swept Sunshine's tail and this started him bucking, which he does in some form, like a Broncho, with arched back and head right down. I shot over his ears and somersaulted, hitting the road an almighty crack with my back and then my head."*

With an injury to her pelvis and spine, it was a couple of weeks at home in bed and the Holland–Martin family were very attentive, with several visits from Mrs Holland-Martin with bundles of books and Jack and Mrs Nicholls calling in. By March and April, point-to-pointing was in full swing with both Thurston and Ruby riding regularly. The highlight was the Worcestershire point-to-point at Chaddesley Corbett.

Ruby Holland-Martin, a consummate horseman in many disciplines, later to become Governor of the Bank of England.

"Hefty has won the Dudley Cup – a thing which the Holland-Martins have never before achieved, even in peace-time with dozens of racehorses. Graham was foisted on to me for the day, which I didn't altogether relish for I loathe anyone tagging at my heels."

Graham was Jack Nicholl's son and it seems not a great favourite of Daphne's. Not long afterwards, on a day described as *"a very hard day when it rained incessantly,"* she continues:

"I was drenched by now, and on my return was ordered by Jack to catch Shag for

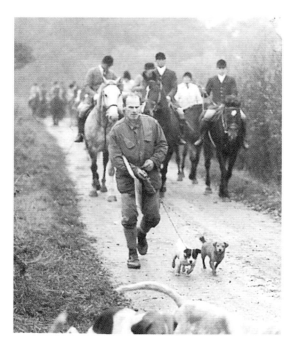

Charles Parker, when terrierman at the Heythrop.

Graham to ride to-night. I really felt that this was a little too much: Why on earth shouldn't the brat catch his own pony, for he comes back from school at 4.30?"

It is interesting to note that 'the brat' became an exceptional rider, working for Peter Cazalet, the Queen Mother's trainer, in Kent, and later returning to Fred Rimell in Worcestershire where he was a sought-after work rider, riding regularly as a jockey.

Daphne was now asking permission for days off to go otterhunting again. In May 1946 at a meet of the Hawkstone she notes, *"By 10.30 the van arrived, with Stallard, George Knight and a boy called Charles Parker, who is a friend of Ron's who whips-in."*

This is the first mention of the legendary Charles Parker, who worked with Ronnie Wallace for most of his foxhunting career, organising the earthstopping and the terriers. Foxes were above ground and few went to ground when Charles Parker was in charge and he played a huge part in the Wallace success story. He was also an avid otter hunter and no one was better at interpreting the natural signs of where an otter might be found.

By June, Daphne had decided to leave Overbury, but dreaded telling Thurston.

"Waited in apprehension for an interview with Thurston in the library and felt almost sick by the time he came in at last. And then it was all most unsatisfactory for I couldn't give the reason for wanting to leave, and I'm utterly miserable anyhow at the idea of going, so that it was all most unsatisfactory. I nearly wept and I expect he hates me now. It was all left in the air and he said he'd talk to me again – but I said I didn't want to go over it again as it makes me feel sick."

A few weeks later Thurston asked her to stay. *"I have agreed to do so if I can have two months clear before returning and provided Jack wants me."* She did indeed return, but hunting had once again become her priority and on 2nd November 1946 Daphne writes:

"My last day at Overbury, and it was rather horrid leaving. I have a nasty sort of empty feeling now, as though my background had gone – which of course it has. I hate goodbyes and it's all been a wrench after 2½ years of the place."

So ended another chapter in Daphne's life. There is no doubt that the Holland-Martin family were an important influence and left a lasting impression on Daphne, as had the Coventrys before. It would not be long before Badminton took over.

CHAPTER NINE

Hunting Resurrected

It was 1947 before Daphne was hunting regularly again and the latter part of that season was to be severely curtailed by heavy snow and the coldest temperatures to be experienced for many years, before or since. Her brother John and his wife Lucile, who had married in 1944, were living nearby and featured regularly in her diary.

In early January Daphne had a day with the Berkeley. *"I have never seen the Berkeley hounds in action – only in kennel and walking out – so I made up my mind to have a day with them today. They meet at the kennels every week at 11.15. It was bitterly cold and more cold weather is forecast, so I felt it was up to me to get today's*

hunting at least. At 11.15 the Joint Masters appeared in their yellow coats." This would have been Captain Robert Berkeley and Major "Chetty" (pronounced "Chatty") Hilton-Green, who had been the legendary Master and amateur huntsman of the Cottesmore before and during the War, although he was on active service for the duration.

On the way to North Africa, the ship he was on was torpedoed. A destroyer came to the rescue, and, as Chetty was being hauled up on to the deck, the sailor who was helping him said: "I thought it was about time you had your second horse, Sir!" It turned out that this man had been one of his

101

whippers-in before the war! However, having had the extraordinary skills to hunt hounds in High Leicestershire before the war, keeping several hundred well-mounted horsemen at bay, and yet allowing his hounds to hunt and kill foxes in style, he never settled after the war and was only at the Berkeley for one season, moving from Hunt to Hunt before eventually retiring to live in Badminton village.

However, this day was to prove a bit of a let-down for Daphne.

"I'm probably a bad judge, but was a little disappointed in "Chetty" Hilton-Green, who didn't strike me as being such a Heaven-born huntsman as his reputation led me to believe. He lifted hounds a great deal, perhaps of necessity, he really had no chance of showing his huntsman's prowess, for the foxes were such ringing ones, and just couldn't run in a straight line."

Daphne's social life was not going anywhere either. Ruby Holland-Martin had telephoned to offer her two Hunt Ball tickets, as he had an injured knee. *"I accepted gratefully, but can't think who to take. I want to ask Bay Parry, but opposition at home."*

The following day she notes:

"I had a nice letter from Bay this morning – funny, when I have been thinking of him, and wanting to ask him down for the Ball. He hopes that I am "happy hunting and well fed – healthy and persistently loved by handsome and wealthy admirers...."!

Dear Bay, there are no handsome or wealthy admirers in this place, just no one at all, not even anyone to take me to a Ball. I am miserable, for I would like to ask Bay, but parental opposition is too strong. I suppose I shall not go at all, for I would rather not go than go with anyone dull or uncongenial."

The 'heaven-born' amateur huntsman of the Cottesmore (1931–1946), Major 'Chetty' Hilton-Green, with his Field Master, Lord Sefton.

morrow. In Evesham there is a depth of 12 feet and there are 16 feet at Birdlip. The evening papers tells of 500 vehicles on the road by Puesdown Inn, where there are drifts up to 20 feet. Sixty five people are stranded there and have to stay at the pub."

But the following day:

"Bill Scott rang up this evening. They have been hunting today! He didn't let me know as I couldn't have got there – but how I wish I had been out. They had a good hunt of 25 minutes in the open; killed one fox and lost the other. He said they were riding over the hedge tops and I can believe it! They really are enterprising. Cheltenham Races are postponed until the week of 16th. The snow is absurdly deep; I struggled down to the town with Ma this afternoon, but the going was awful."

Nevertheless, she was foxhunting six days a week on foot and this week she went to the Duke of Beaufort's on Monday, the Croome on Tuesday, the Duke of Beaufort's again on Wednesday, the Warwickshire on Thursday, the Ledbury on Friday and the North Cotswold on Saturday. Her last day's hunting before the snow was on January 21st and then hunting became impossible. By March, only the North Cotswold, with Bill Scott as Master and Huntsman, tried to hunt in the snow.

On March 5th it was still snowing and Daphne writes, *"the snow which continued all night is still falling. I have never seen anything like it, and if it continues at this rate, we shan't get out of the door to-*

Meanwhile, having given up employment and struggling to get more work writing, Daphne was finding herself rather short of funds.

She wrote to Pip Stanier, Secretary of the Hawkstone Otterhounds to say that she must resign as a subscriber. However, she received a letter back:

Dear Daphne,
I was most distressed to get your letter. Finance is a great worry to most people in these days. But my dear Daph you cannot resign after 1st of Jan. I brought your case up at the committee meeting

The 10th Duke of Beaufort in 1950. Known as 'Master' to all his friends, he gained his nickname when he hunted a small pack of harriers that his father gave him as a boy and he would be asked, "Where are you going to draw next, Master?"

and the committee told me to write you a nice letter which I am endeavouring to do: to say that for all you have done for the Hunt they would waive your sub, so come out and say nothing, in uniform when you can. I shall be hunting hounds quite a few days at the start of the season. My best love, Pip

However it was 1949 before Daphne wrote her next full otterhunting diary, although meanwhile she had plenty of days with the Hawkstone described in her main foxhunting diary. It was petrol rationing that limited the number of meets she could reach.

But back to 1947 and Daphne, with her small car, was able to reach the Beaufort. So far, she had always found the kennel-huntsman, Ted Read, hunting hounds, but at the end of March, following the thaw, she went to the meet at Old Sodbury to find *"to my joy the Duke was hunting hounds and at long last I had the pleasure of seeing him. He looked beautiful on a horse – like a centaur.*

Only Ted whipped-in; I believe the other whipper-in is ill. It was the turn of the bitch pack, about 15½ couple according to my reckoning. Waspish from the N. Cotswold was amongst them. The Duke pointed her out to me later.

Several small coverts were drawn blank, and the field followed some distance behind, whilst I ran with hounds and the Duke. A very dead sheep's carcass proved rather too attractive to hounds and he asked me to put them away from it, and I swelled with pride!

I regard him (as the leading M.F.H. of the Country) as a kind of God, to be held in awe and devotion, and when, later, he told me I was very useful (having opened gates and rated hounds away from the carcass!) I felt once more swollen with pride."

During the day she talked to a farmer who she had met out with the Berkeley: *"He told me that Major Hilton-Green has departed from the Berkeley – horses and all! Later another Berkeley*

farmer told me the same tale. I wonder WHO he has gone with this time!!" – and then added in different ink, clearly at a later date – *"It proved to be Myrtle Berkeley, his Joint Master's wife!!"*

After a busy day, they ran back to the Park at Badminton, where the fox was killed and Daphne was given the brush. At the end of the day Daphne enquired of the Duke the way to Old Sodbury. *"He asked the car followers en masse who could give me a lift, which I thought very nice of him."*

From now on Daphne was clearly smitten by the 10th Duke of Beaufort, his hounds, and Badminton.

A few days later Daphne was back for another spring day.

"I hadn't expected the Duke to be hunting hounds today, so I was more than delighted when he appeared with his bitch pack. There was a black-and-tan bitch out today and I asked the Duke about her; he told me that she comes from Jock Jardine of the Dumfriesshire and when I asked if she went back to Croome Clansman, he said yes, she did, so I felt very pleased. I also screwed up my courage and requested to be allowed to go to kennels and see hounds one day. He said that I may."

The Duke would have been surprised that this new, keen, foot follower had such a knowledge and interest in hounds.

Indeed, after two more April days with the Beaufort, *"I summoned up all my courage – and it needed a good deal! – and rang up His Grace the Duke of Beaufort to ask if I might go over to the kennels this week. I expected an underling to answer – but it proved to be the Duke himself. He*

52

NOVEMBER 6th.

(Opening Meet.)

SOUTHWICK PARK

(with the Arle Court Harriers.)

" It is our Opening Day"

I had a lot of fun to-day – more jumping than in an average day's foxhunting. And old Leicester went better than ever before.

Just as I was going across to saddle him up I met George Goodwin, who was on his way to Southwick. Collie was mounting him & he was going to whip-in. I always like George. I hadn't seen him since the Croome Puppy Show.

I was early at the meet, & one of the men took my horse & I went indoors for a drink. There was a field of about 15 altogether — Mrs. Unwin, Gersham & Joyce & young Diana, the Parrys, Maguire, Charlie Chatham, Mr. Leared (the deaf man), young Pullen, & a couple of people whose names I don't know. Mr. Lulham, George & Rags were whipping-in. Mrs. Lulham, Mrs. Lewis, Dr. Bower, Mr. & Mrs. Tim Unwin & their child, & various farmers & people were also there. Collie always provides a proper hunt breakfast for the farmers at the Opening Meet, & there are always a lot on foot.

A photographer from the Chronicle & Graphic was then taking photos, & Tim Unwin borrowed a drawing horn & blew a few blasts to make hounds show themselves nicely.

Eventually, at about 11·30, we moved off, but it was 12·0 or after when hounds put up their first hare, somewhere near Mr. Chidley's, I think.

OPENING MEET
Arle Court Harriers At Southwick Park

The opening meet of the Arle Court Harriers was held on Friday at the residence of the master, Mr. W. C. Unwin, Southwick Park, near Tewkesbury.

Mr. and Mrs. Unwin welcomed all their friends with their usual hospitality, and the local farmers were entertained to a sit-down breakfast. Among others present were Mrs. R. Donaldson, Mr. E. R. Milner, Miss Daphne Moore, Miss N. Newman, Mr. C. E. Pullen, Miss Beryl Parry, Mr. B. Parry, Mr. Gershom Wood, Mrs. Wood and Dinah, Mr. Wilfred N. Unwin, Timothy Unwin. Mr. C. Chatham, Mr. and Mrs. D. G. Chidley. Mr. T. Marston, Mr. C. Gibbons. Mr. and Mrs. W. Smith, Mr. W. Davis, Mr. and Mrs. M. Lulham, Dr. J. Bower (field master), Mr. G. Goodwin, Mr. J. H. Leared, Mr. W. Billings, Mr. W. Oakev and Mrs. C. Lewis.

A page from Daphne's diary – her neat handwriting was never crossed out or amended and was often embellished with her distinctive watercolours, photos and newspaper cuttings.

was very nice and although he says he won't be there on Tuesday (which is disappointing) Ted will show me the hounds."

Walking out in the Park with the doghounds, *"there was a herd of deer grazing quite close to us, but the hounds never took the least notice of them – young 'uns and all were as steady as rocks."* She makes detailed notes of the stallion hounds in her diary and says, *"as usual, I preferred the bitches to the doghounds and I liked some of those by South & West Wilts sires"* [these would have been of Ikey Bell's breeding] *"and thought they had very good necks and shoulders. The Beaufort type is far heavier. I know they hunt quite magnificently, but it isn't the type which I have been brought up on and to me they seem too big and stuffy."*

This would soon change at Badminton as the Duke became more influenced by the Masters who were breeding a more active type of hound along the lines that George Coventry had always advocated.

Daphne's next kennel visit was to the Warwickshire.

"George Gillson, probably the best and most popular professional huntsman living, showed us hounds. He knows me as The Lady Who Runs! I was certainly treated by everyone as a far more important person than I deserved! For three solid hours we

stood on the flags looking at hounds. I loved the way George showed his hounds; they came out happy and trustful, obviously adoring him.

He is a nice little man, and, I am told, an artist in the field. The bitches were, I thought, better than the dogs, who were, to my mind, on the heavy side. Generally I do prefer bitches. The Young Entry of bitches were a wonderfully level, well matched lot, and despite the fact that the majority were by Puckeridge Woodcock (a very big dog I am told,) they are full of quality and not the least bit coarse. Only the lighter, more "quality" bitches had been put to him, and the results justified the experiment.

I have been brought up to like the lightish, galloping type of doghound and thought that these had too much lumber, but of course I do know that it is easy to get hounds too light and "shelly" and lose that vital attribute – CONSTITUTION. But I still prefer my first love as a type."

Daphne's last day with the Beaufort that season was on May 1st, which shows how different farming must have been in those days to enable a large field of horsemen to cross the country so late in the year. Less than four months later they were hunting again – and Daphne was out!

After a busy summer of otterhunting, hound shows and puppy

The 10th Duke of Beaufort pictured in 1925. Daphne was in seventh heaven when he and the Duchess invited her to stay the night at Badminton.

shows, on 23rd August 1948 Daphne climbed into her car at 4am to drive to Badminton for the first morning's cubhunting. Stowed in the back and carefully packed in layers of paper and a cardboard box was the Stud Book, which the Duke had commissioned Daphne to write, featuring all his current hounds, in her immaculate script and with their pedigrees carefully

checked by her in the annual *Foxhound Kennel Studbook*. The Duke had asked Daphne to undertake this task when he invited her to the Puppy Show earlier in the summer. Following Lord Knutsford across country to the draw, she *"feared for the springs of my poor little car"* until eventually an ominous thud realised her worse fears.

However, the mixed pack, hunted by Ted Read, *"ran with such a chorus that the trees almost shook with the echoes of it. Round and round they drove, one fox (probably an old one) slipping away and cubs being viewed on all sides."*

With a brace killed it was decided to finish. *"Master had invited me to breakfast at Badminton, during a lull in proceedings, and naturally I was overjoyed. The Stud Book was well received. The Duchess (who had been out on a big brown horse side-saddle) was an absolute dear and there were three adorable dogs. We had bacon and eggs and peaches, and altogether everything was perfect. Master now had to dash off to the Estate Office – he never has any rest – and I prepared to leave.*

He asked me when I was coming down again, and, to my uttermost bliss, the Duchess invited me to come and stay at Badminton next week. Tuesday to hunt Wednesday. She said I could go to-morrow for Monday, but as I have promised

Mrs Lewis to go with her otterhunting to Crickhowell, I can't let her down."

On Monday, following a long day with the otterhounds, Daphne returned to find a wire saying:

"Expecting you to-night. Beaufort."
Naturally it was impossible to get there at that time of night and I nearly died of misery and despair. Mamma had wisely wired back: "Daphne otterhunting in Wales. Will phone on her return," so I rang Master and he has asked me for Thursday night instead. So now I have 3 more days to live through somehow…

You will note that Daphne now refers to the Duke as "Master," which all his friends called him. He gained this nickname when he hunted a small pack of harriers that his father gave him as a boy and he would be asked, *"where are we going to draw next, Master?"*

Eventually Thursday arrived. *"Thank God, I'm here at last! I am in the room which Master had as a boy and it is full of photos of him in the uniform of the Eton College Beagles and at the Royal Military College. I love it. And my landing is full of the most exciting hunting pictures, so that I wonder I ever got to bed to-night. I*

Major Dick Fanshawe, Joint Master and huntsman of the North Cotswold, moving off from the Lygon Arms in Broadway at the Opening Meet 1951.

love being here beyond words. The Duchess and I went to the kitchen gardens in search of peaches soon after my arrival. We were accompanied by numerous dogs which are always at the Duchess's heels." She then describes all the dogs individually – no less than fourteen of them! *"Nobody bothers to change for dinner, and after dinner we just sat and talked and I looked at my Peterborough article in the* Chronicle of America *(I was rather horrified to find that they have it here; I thought I should be safe from the critical eye of English Masters!) and went to bed."*

"Today we met at The Verge – close to kennels – at 6.0am. Master called me at 5.15, and about 5.30 we all assembled on the landing below for bread and butter and tea. The Duchess was hunting on foot, bringing the terriers, so I went with her to the kennels to fetch two of the terriers from there and we went together. Ted put the mixed pack in at the Verge and they soon found, but obviously there wasn't much scent."

After finally catching a cub, they walked back to the house for breakfast…*"and then the Duchess turned me loose on the sporting pictures and I was enthralled by what she showed me. Later on the Duchess showed me a stuffed wolf in a glass case, which was hunted by the 8th Duke's hounds, who were invited to France for the purpose of wolf-hunting in a forest there. Whilst I was gazing at the pictures*

Master came in and asked me if I would care to stay to-night and they would find me a horse on which to go cubhunting in the morning? Would I care to…! I was almost crazy with joy, not only at the idea of riding after so long – but just to be staying in this paradise an extra day. Later I went round the livestock with the Duchess. She works like a navvy with them, in old dungarees or a torn brown overall; a grand person she is. She has cows (a special breed known as Gloucesters), goats, rabbits, ducks, hens, cats, kittens, dogs without number, ever a 52-year-old donkey!"

After another good morning's cubhunting with Master hunting his bitches, Daphne returned to Tewkesbury stating, *"I have NEVER had such a heavenly time."*

The following day Daphne bicycled to Overbury. With petrol still rationed, she had to save it for her ever-increasing trips to Badminton. There she fetched Thurston's Stud Book to be written up and also writes, *"sent off Glog Nimrod's pedigree to Master who hasn't got it and I was proud and thrilled to be able to supply it."*

Her reputation as an expert on the pedigrees of both hounds and horses was developing and Master was to increasingly rely on her knowledge and drafting skills. Her visits to the Beaufort country continued, sometimes staying at Badminton House and on other occasions with Mr Butt, a Badminton tenant, the Castles, and the whipper-in, Bert Pateman. She made herself even more indispensable by doing secretarial work for Mary Beaufort and the earthstopping cards for Master.

In January 1948 the Duke of Beaufort's hounds had a very good hunt from Great Wood. One of the most famous hunts in history had been from this same covert in 1871, when hounds ran for three and a half hours, covering 27 miles, with a furthest point of 16 miles over three hunting countries. The 23-year-old Marquess of Worcester, Master's father and later the ninth Duke of Beaufort, was hunting hounds.

The fox took them from their own country, across the VWH, crossing the River Thames twice, and into the Old Berks Country, where he was marked to ground in a drain under the vicarage garden at Highworth. The young huntsman completed the hunt on a cob borrowed from a local farmer; hounds and remaining horses boarded a special train at Swindon, which took them back to Chippenham, the nearest station to Badminton then.

On Daphne's day, when she followed on foot and by car, Ted Read was hunting hounds from the meet at Dauntsey as Master was laid up after a fall. The first fox from Great Wood was killed after a 35-minute hunt and hounds returned to Great Wood to draw again.

"Now began a second historic 'Great Wood Run', not quite so momentous as the one of 1871, but a great achievement all the same. Hounds spoke to a fox on re-entering the covert and Major Gundry (then Hunt Secretary) turned to me and said 'what's the time?' It was then 12.45. Ten minutes later the fox was holloaed away at the same corner as the previous one, but this time swung left, pointing for the brook and VWH Cricklade country."

After following the hoofprints for a while, Daphne was lucky enough to be picked up by followers in a car, who knew the country well.

"Hounds were running on hard, a good deal of the time alone, for no-one could keep with them, and moreover, there was a considerable amount of wire in the Cricklade country. Roughly, after crossing Brinkworth Brook at the railway, they went through the Shrubs and the Folly to Ballard's Ash, on by Flaxlands and Lydiard's Plain, leaving Red Lodge Wood on their left, to Purton

The Beaufort Hunt move off from the meet at Acton Turville on the occasion of the visit of Prince Bernhard of the Netherlands. Daphne can be seen far right on foot with the terriers Spot and Rip.

Princess Margaret, pictured with the Duchess of Beaufort, on her first day's hunting in the spring of 1949 with the Duke of Beaufort's hounds.

Stoke Common and eventually reached Blakehill Aerodrome at Chelworth Farm.

It was now 2.0 o'clock and until then they hadn't had a single real check. When we reached them Ted was casting very carefully up and down a ditch on the Aerodrome. It seems that the fox was viewed just in front of hounds after crossing the runway towards this ditch, but Ted thought it best to leave hounds to themselves as they had done it all themselves up till now. Later, he blamed himself for not lifting them, for the fox unaccountably vanished into thin air and presumably found his way into some culvert or other. It was terribly hard luck on both Ted and his hounds.

Anyway, it was a wonderful hunt and I was remarkably lucky to be there at the finish. The point measured 8½ miles and hounds had run pretty well in a straight line."

Daphne was now hunting most days with the Beaufort and, more often than not, was asked to take the terriers, with Master often bringing them to the meet for her. However, not every day went well for Daphne.

It would not have been easy to follow the Beaufort hounds on foot with two terriers, when they covered so much country. From a meet at Hullavington, where Mary Beaufort had given her a lift with the terriers, Spot and Rip, she found it

"...very wet and flooded everywhere now and the going is bad for me. Today, moreover, a howling gale is raging and this made it very difficult to keep in touch with hounds. It was a rotten day from my point of view and I returned in the depths of misery and despair."

Having lost touch with hounds, she eventually heard that they were on their way home.

"*So I reluctantly turned again for Sherston, very weary and very sick at heart. It's no use for me to take the terriers if I'm not there when required. Twice today the dogs were needed and I wasn't there. I was feeling completely miserable at having been so useless today and do hope that I shall be allowed to run the terriers another time.*"

However, a few days later, following a meet at Sevington, she notes: "*Thank Goodness I've been more successful as Terrier Man than last week, and was there today when needed at the end of a long hunt.*"

If proof were needed that foxhunting was truly back in its former glory, following the war, it was the day that Prince Bernhard of the Netherlands stayed at Badminton for a day's hunting in February 1949. Daphne's diary heads the day with a quotation from Masefield: "*We shall talk of today until we die.*" She continues:

"*One of those days which will live forever. How seldom it happens that a day's hunting turns out just as it should when sport is particularly needed…and yet today things could hardly have gone better. It was a wonderful Heaven-sent day, and I'm sure Prince Bernhard enjoyed it. This morning I collected Spot and Rip from the house and set off in good time to walk to the meet at Acton Turville. Crowds of horses passed me on the way, and it was soon obvious that it was going to be an enormous meet, with a huge, hostile, jealous, riding field. There must have been over 300 all told and cars by the dozen. Hounds arrived soon after I did; the bitches of course, with Master hunting them, and Bert and Will whipping-in.*"

Bert Pateman was first whipper-in and Will Ockwell, second whipper-in. "*Press photographers appeared to spring up like mushrooms on all sides and immediately surrounded the unfortunate Prince, who will appear in almost every newspaper in the country tomorrow.*"

Hounds ran magnificently all day, killing a brace "handsomely" after two hunts with points over 4 miles. "*I walked back to Badminton and left the dogs. Prince Bernhard was coming in just as I was going out and said: 'I see you've made it' – he certainly uses idiomatic English very charmingly. I think he thoroughly enjoyed his day and went very well.*"

Spring hunting the same season saw Princess Margaret out with the Beaufort. "*A great day – Princess Margaret's first appearance foxhunting. I was very surprised as I thought she was leaving this morning; she has had a most sporting weekend, going to the Berkeley Point-to-*

Point (where I saw her) on Saturday, seeing both the Beaufort and Berkeley hounds on Sunday, (and Peter Scott's wildfowl sanctuary) and hunting today. It took me no fewer than seven lifts to reach the meet (I decided to hitchhike to save petrol) and five to reach home to-night. The village of Tresham had got wind of the Royal visit and had slung flags from every available cottage window. I had Spot and Rip delivered to me in the van from Badminton, and Rip was so delighted to see me. Photographers abounded and the Princess was photographed from every angle. She rode Jock Scot, Mary's horse, and wore jodhpurs and a tweed coat, and a bowler hat. It was a perfect morning and very warm and sunny – not good for scent, but a glorious day to be out."

The morning was spent in the hills around Foxholes and above Kilcot. Later in the afternoon hounds ran well from Withymore to Lower Woods and right through to Hays Wood.

A month later and Daphne was otterhunting. *"Otterhunting again! And this season I shall be able to go to the meets with hounds – as in the old days at Croome – for they are to be kennelled at Andoversford with the Cotswold Hounds and Ron will drive the van."*

Capt Ronnie Wallace had become Master and Huntsman of the Cotswold Hounds in 1948, remaining Master and Huntsman of the Hawkstone Otterhounds. Petrol rationing had limited Daphne's days with the otterhounds since the end of the war, but now she would be able to travel in the hound van again and she celebrated by starting her annual otterhunting diaries again.

In her summary of the otterhunting season she notes that she has been out 58 days. It could now be said that Daphne's hunting life was full and rewarding again.

CHAPTER TEN

Hunting Further Afield

While the Duke of Beaufort's had become Daphne's 'home' pack, she made use of her regular billet with George Castle and his family near Badminton to extend her interests eastwards and begun to hunt regularly with the V.W.H. (Earl Bathurst's) and the Royal Agricultural College Beagles. During the season 1949-50 she often ran the terriers for the Bathurst as well as those from Badminton.

She made good friends with Lady Apsley from Cirencester Park, whose family owned the hounds and the kennels. Lady Apsley was Master of her family pack from 1946 to 1956, but had been confined to a wheelchair following a serious hunting accident before the war. She was a devoted foxhunter, seldom missed a day, and, driven by her keen hunting chauffeur in a Land Rover, usually saw as much sport as the mounted field.

The original Vale of White Horse Hunt was established in 1831, but in 1835 the Master, Mr Hoare from the banking family, removed his hounds to Cricklade following an appalling hunt row over his relationship with an underage lady. The two hunts remained separated as the V.W.H. (Cricklade) and the V.W.H. (Earl Bathurst's) until the two countries were reunited in 1964. Lady Apsley's father-in-law, the 7th Earl Bathurst, who was Master of his hounds from 1892 until 1943, was an outspoken advocate of the Old English Foxhound and firm opponent of the introduction of Welsh blood.

The 1949 Opening Meet of the V.W.H. (Earl Bathurst's) hounds was at Bibury Court.

"A very exciting and eventful day, for me at least. I started as Terrier Man, was promoted to Hunt second horseman, and finished up on the Whipper-in's horse, following hounds over a nice line of country.

It happened like this: The huntsman Joe Wright's horse cut a vein early on in the first hunt and was sent home in a box with Ted Goddard (who was out as second whipper-in) who handed his mare to Joe. Then Jean Russell-Perkins, riding Lady Apsley's liver chestnut mare – which has

The Duke of Beaufort's doghounds, hunted by Ted Read (left) meet at Cirencester Park by invitation of the Vale of the White Horse Hunt (VWH Lord Bathurst) in March 1950. The Duke is on the right in the 'blue and buff' Beaufort livery.

The Royal Agricultural College Beagles Opening Meet at the College during the Mastership of Mike Ardagh, a good friend of Daphne's, in 1949.

been ridden by Joe during the cubhunting — had a fall and broke or dislocated her finger and was driven home. I had been driving round with Lady Apsley in the Land Rover with the terrier, Nettle, and now took over Jean's mare, so that I could ride second horse to Joe. When I handed her over I had the bay mare and Lady Apsley said I could go on with her and have a hunt. So I did. As I had no hat I swore I wouldn't jump anything, but of course when hounds found and went away, I went too. We had plenty to jump, all nice clean fences or walls, with no wire. At the end of the day I handed the mare over to the groom and walked back to the house for a very welcome tea. I am staying to-night and hunt with the Beagles tomorrow."

After spending the night at Cirencester Park, the splendid home of the Bathurst family, which is divided from the town by an enormous yew hedge of world record height and overlooking the Park on the other side,

119

The Duke of Beaufort hunting his bitch pack in 1959.

Daphne met the R.A.C. Beagles at Tarlton. *"A very hard day indeed, with too many hares and a lot of plough. We were running almost without cessation and the poor whippers-in had a very tough time of it. The Master must have very nearly died of exhaustion..."*

At the end of her day's diary she notes, *"Charles Parker was, to my great surprise, out today, arriving, like a millionaire, by taxi, but looking like nothing on earth but a scarecrow! He swore me to secrecy; it seems that he should have been* earthstopping instead and undoubtedly he was wearing his earthstopper's clothes!" Charles Parker was Ronnie Wallace's right hand man at the Ludlow, the Cotswold

Brilliant hound breeder, Sir Newton Rycroft, with his Dummer Beagles in Gloucestershire in 1950.

and the Heythrop, doing most of the earthstopping, but strangely never had a driving licence. Mike Ardagh, a student at Cirencester College, was hunting the beagles this season. He was clearly a good friend of Daphne's, and she wrote their reports for *Horse and Hound*.

A few day's later it was the Duke of Beaufort's Opening Meet from Tormarton.

"A most eventful day for almost everybody, and an alarming number of falls to start the Season Proper. In fact, this evening at tea, Master remarked ghoulishly that there was "blood on every wall"! What a dangerous game foxhunting is!

I came down in the car yesterday (Sunday) afternoon, having picked up Mike Ardagh outside the Agricultural College at Cirencester, lunched with him at the Hare & Hounds, and proceeded to the Badminton kennels where we walked out in the Park with hounds.

I rang up Master on Saturday evening for permission and found him in tremendous form, having had the hunt of a lifetime from the Foxley Green meet, to finish the so-called cubhunting. Hounds had achieved a hunt of some eighteen miles, with a furthest point of eight miles, only the Duke being up with hounds when they killed their fox. Not one of the field had survived to the end."

Two and a half couple of the extremely level Dummer Beagle bitches.

Daphne hunted with several other packs of beagles that season, including the Dummer and the Warwickshire, as well as most of the nearby packs of foxhounds, including the Ledbury, the Cotswold, the Cotswold Farmers, the Croome and the North Cotswold, about whom she was very disparaging.

"Jimmy Delmege is back, temporarily from Canada, and was acting as Field Master. He greeted me genially as Daphne – but he really has behaved in the most extraordinary manner, and I wonder he wasn't thrown out of the M.F.H. Association. He took on the Mastership again for this season, and then rushed off to Canada, where he bought a ranch, leaving his K.H to hunt hounds (which, as far as I know, he had never done before); returned to live at the Lygon Arms – whilst his nice wife lives 2 miles away at Little Buckland! – and is usually out on a hunting day in a jeep, driving madly across country and heading the foxes. It is all most peculiar… it's not like hunting with the North Cotswold in Bill Scott's day!"

It was during this season that Daphne first met Newton Rycroft and his Dummer Beagles. Later in his life, as Sir Newton Rycroft, he became one of the most brilliant – if somewhat unorthodox – breeders of foxhounds while Master of the New Forest.

He was brought up at Dummer, in Hampshire, where both his father and grandfather had been Master of the Vine Foxhounds. A brilliant classical scholar, educated at Winchester and Oxford, he started his private pack of beagles immediately on coming down from university aged twenty one. As an intellectual, his unusual and scientific outlook on hound breeding, totally unhindered by fashion or tradition, may have raised a few eyebrows, but he succeeded in breeding the almost perfect level, quality pack of beagle bitches.

Daphne's sketch of John Jorrocks MFH, the Surtees character depicting the sporting cockney grocer.

After a distinguished army career during the war, he returned to set up home in Gloucestershire and develop his pack of beagles in the Heythrop country, where they hunt to this day. Many people thought him eccentric,

Portman Lovelock '47, pictured at their Bryanston kennels, and Champion Doghound at Honiton Show, as described by Daphne.

which he certainly was, but Daphne was most impressed with her first couple of days with him.

"They are practically all light coloured; all bitches save one dog, Woldsman, now in his 9th season. They are small, but amazingly active, with beautiful necks and shoulders to enable them to get over the Cotswold stone walls. The Master believes in letting hounds hunt themselves – which they do with remarkable success, and whilst watching their every move, is not above conversing at intervals. I thus discovered that he is a "Welsh-cross" enthusiast and most knowledgeable on the pedigrees which I have been brought up on (Curre, Brecon, etc)."

Later that spring, Daphne visited the Dummer kennels. *"I picked up Mike (Ardagh) in Cheltenham and we drove on to Little Rissington, where we saw the pack in kennels and walked out with them up the road. Newton has taught them a new trick, namely, to sit in a row across the lane, looking very maidenly and prim, whilst he and Bill walk on. Then, after going some distance, he turns round and calls each by name, whilst the others remain seated! They really are marvellously disciplined."*

Writing later in *Horse & Hound*, Daphne describes the kennel discipline.

"A visit to these kennels is a joy. Bill Porter always has his charges in first class condition, their coats clean and shining, their kennels

spotless; and the discipline of the pack is a revelation. Cheerful obedience is the keynote; they are gay and lively yet ready to obey the least command. "Stand still"! they are told, and they remain motionless but alert, unattended in field or lane until their master's call releases them and they race helter-skelter to his side.

There is no doubt that this little pack combines both looks and performance, for these hounds show magnificent sport and are an education to watch in the field. Scientifically bred and very ably handled by their Master, they are in the front rank of present day beagles and will undoubtedly go down to history."

The summer was a short one.

"It hasn't really been long since we were last foxhunting – at Marshfield Rocks with the Beaufort on May 1st. And most of the summer I have been at Puppy Shows or Hound Shows, with a bit of otterhunting." Bill Scott was now a Master of the Portman, sharing the hunting of the hounds with Sir Peter Farquhar.

"I went down to stay with the Bill Scotts for Honiton Hound Show, getting a lift with Ron and Valerie Wallace, and arriving (rather late!) for dinner. To our great joy the Portman won the Doghound Championship with their lovely dog, Lovelock '47. They also won the Entered Couple Class (doghounds) and the Stallion

Major Dick Fanshawe, Joint Master and huntsman of the North Cotswold, and a firm favourite of Daphne's, with hounds at their Broadway kennels in 1951.

Hound Class – so there was champagne all round at dinner."

There was another house party at the Farquhars' house at Turnworth, near Blandford, including Col. "Peach" Borwick, Master of the Pytchley, Major Maurice Barclay, Master of the Puckeridge and Sir John Buchanan-Jardine, Master of the Dumfriesshire.

"So it was a distinguished field of M.F.H's for this initial morning's

cubhunting. We rode to the meet with hounds... this always makes my day. It was the bitch pack, which Peter hunts, and

Daphne with Sir Peter Farquhar, one of the greatest hound breeders of his time, at a meet of the Duke of Beaufort's hounds in the 1970s.

the coverts behind the house were drawn and hounds soon found, but there wasn't a great deal of scent. After a busy morning and a brace killed, it was decided to go home. We rode back with hounds, had a second breakfast at the pub at Blandford, and then spent a blissful morning in kennels

with the Experts. Some of Bill's rather more unorthodox hounds possibly shook the purist soul of Major Barclay, but there are some lovely hounds in the Portman pack which he could not fail to admire. After lunch we returned sleepily in the Wallaces' car to Gloucestershire – and so home."

Daphne was now meeting all the important people in the foxhunting world and, as a result of the Portman visit, she was invited to see the famed Pytchley hounds by their Master, "Peach" Borwick.

The huntsman was Stanley Barker, who took over from the legendary Frank Freeman in 1931 and hunted the Pytchley until 1960.

"Though not hunting, this must be included in my diary, for it was such a remarkable occasion – my first view of the Pytchley. I have, of course, seen individual hounds at Peterborough, but I was very lucky to be able to see the whole pack in kennels with such a hound expert as Colonel Borwick. They are, like Masefield's, "A lovely pack for looks," and I imagine that their working qualities are as good as their looks. Colonel Borwick invited me to Haselbech in time for lunch; we were then to spend the afternoon in kennels with Stanley Barker and I was to stay the night at Haselbech.

Stanley is an artist at showing hounds; he had no whipper-in to help him and though he entered the yard with a whip in his hand, this was soon thrown on to the ground, where it remained for the rest of the visit!"

She describes the hounds she saw in detail and finishes by saying; *"I came away with a general impression of grand backs and good shoulders – and of hounds most beautifully shown."*

On her way home, Daphne called at the Warwickshire kennels for a cup of tea with George Gillson and then at the North Cotswold kennels where she walked out with hounds and had tea with the Fanshawes. Major Dick Fanshawe was the new Master and had taken over after the three disastrous seasons of Jimmy Delmege, who had got rid of most of the hounds bred by Bill Scott.

Sir Newton Rycroft, Master of the New Forest Foxhounds, when he was no longer hunting hounds himself in 1976.

"Now that the obnoxious Delmege has gone and most of his Old Berks. Bullocks, and now that Dicky Fanshawe and David

Lt. Colonel Dick Eames hunting his white West Country Cotley Harriers. He rode with a stiff leg following a war injury.

Mitchell are Masters and are building up a new pack on the right lines, I shall look forward to several days with them this season."

Indeed it was only a few days before she did just that.

"Dick Fanshawe hunted his entire pack this morning – 40 couple of them – in that Pinch-me-near-Forest known as Lidcombe Wood. It's a villainous place at the best of times, but with a large pack of draft hounds, mainly quite unknown quantities, it is a huntsman's nightmare. Anyhow, they succeeded in finding and hunting a considerable number of cubs with their hounds from the Beaufort, the Berkeley, the Portman, Lady Curre's, Miss Guest's, the South Dorset, the Pytchley, the Cricklade, and a few North Cotswold (Delmege vintage), whilst one or two of Bill Scott's old North Cotswold still remain."

Jack Stallard, 1st whipper-in and kennel-huntsman, leading the Hawkstone Otterhounds from a meet at Pontrilas, Herefordshire, after the war, with Ronnie Wallace hunting hounds.

Sir Peter Farquhar, pictured in 1958, hunting his Portman bitches.

who won the Harrier Championship. Though originally harriers, the Cotley, in time, began to hunt foxes as well; more recently fox was hunted entirely and the Cotley were recognised by the MFHA.

Hounds are mainly harrier-bred, and in the Harrier and Beagle Stud Book, though lately College Valley blood has been introduced. The harrier blood is pure West Country of the best type; hounds are white, with lemon and badger-pie markings, glorious clean necks and shoulders for the most part – and HARE FOOTED."

The following morning the meet was at Monkton Wyld…

"and Wyld was the right name, for it is a very jungly district. I went in the Land Rover with Joan (Mrs Eames), who doesn't ride, but has brought the art of car-following to a fine art. The terriers go in a box at the back, the tools are packed into their allocated space, lunch hangs from the sides, nothing is forgotten or left out.

I found such efficiency almost terrifying. We picked up two girls, Norman Bartlett, who runs the terriers (and later was Master and huntsman of the Culmstock otterhounds) and two other men.

By now the Land Rover was more or less full to capacity. The Master, Colonel Dick Eames hunted hounds, riding with a stiff leg due to a war wound, with Tom Healy, his

Later that autumn, Daphne visited another important and unique pack of hounds on the Dorset, Devon & Somerset borders, the Cotley. These white West Country Harriers are synonymous with the name of the Eames family. The hunt was founded in 1797, in the reign of George III, and a member of the Eames family has been Master ever since.

"I have been interested in the Cotley for some time and at this year's Peterborough was much struck by their beautiful Ringlet

Lt. Colonel Dick Eames with his pack of Cotley Harriers, described by Daphne as the 'White Wonders of the West.'

kennel-huntsman, whipping-in. His cousin, David Eames, also whipped-in as well as a couple of sporting farmers all wearing the green coats of the Cotley. Most of those out, mounted or on foot, were puppy walkers and immensely keen. I loved the way they knew the hounds, as no doubt their fathers and grandfathers did before them."

"There were 18½ couple of hounds and they provided a series of hunts which convinced me of their quite astonishing drawing powers. They are very high couraged, pushing their way through impenetrable undergrowth to force their fox away. There is no hanging about in the rides; the undergrowth shakes as they push their way through, but save for this there might not be a hound for miles — until they speak. When they do, you can bet your bottom dollar there is a fox there. Their cry is high pitched, not, I thought, particularly melodious, but quite carrying. Dusk had fallen when we finished the day, and bats were flittering to and fro and the distant view of the sea towards Charmouth faded as the light gradually died."

Daphne was totally enthused by the new Mastership of Dick Fanshawe at the North Cotswold and the task he was undertaking, with such skill, of restoring the standard of the pack to what they had been in Bill Scott's day.

He had previously been Master of the South Oxfordshire and, while he had been away at the War, his wife Ruth, a sister of Sir Peter Farquhar, had not only run the Hunt, but had hunted hounds herself. It was not surprising that the Fanshawes became firm friends of Daphne's and that season she spent as many days with the North Cotswold as she did with the Beaufort. Their Opening Meet was, as always, at the Lygon Arms in Broadway, opposite the kennels.

"It was a very smart Opening Meet this morning with a lot of scarlet coats and plenty of spit-and-polish. Very nice to see and sadly missing in the Croome and Ledbury these days. The weather was perfect and

Bay de Courcy Parry, better known as 'Dalesman', in old age at Rydal Show, presenting a cup to Edmund Porter, Master of the Eskdale and Ennerdale fell pack.

there was a vast crowd of foot-people outside the Lygon, completely surrounding hounds and Hunt Staff. Dick and Albert [Albert Buckle, his kennel-huntsman and first whipper-in, who later had such an illustrious career as huntsman of the Whaddon Chase under the Mastership of Dorian Williams] *were resplendent in their new red coats, but the yellow collars are hard to get now and they wore plain scarlet."*

A very busy day for hounds was clearly full of other incidents. *"The Hunting Editor of the Field, Colonel Smith-Maxwell, fell into (sic) his hat and so jangled his brains that he was subsequently seen riding down the railway, without, I think, any idea as to how he got on, or, more importantly should a train appear, how he could get off.*

He departed shortly after they killed their first fox, somewhat the worse for wear, and moaning about his poor battered head. There was a good deal of jumping and a great many "voluntaries" – including, to my unholy delight, Ruby Holland-Martin!

Captain Evetts mounted a haystack with the express purpose of roaring at the field, whom he suspected of riding over his precious wheat. I had never heard such a terrifying noise in all my life!" The day ended, as most days did with the North Cotswold... *"and I stayed to tea with the Fanshawes."*

Dick Fanshawe continued to show good sport throughout that season and the following Opening Meet Daphne repeated:

"A very successful Opening Meet; a really busy day with a good hunt and a kill in the open. The photographers Meads – pere et fils – were out, young Meads running like a stag all day and always being in the right place."

Jim Meads and his father Frank are world famous for their hunting photography. Jim now in his eighties, is known as "the running photographer" and has hunted with no less than 501 different packs on both sides of the Atlantic.

73

AUGUST

"Dry August and warm
Doth Harvest no harm."

(THOMAS TUSSER - "August's Husbandry".)

Captain Ronnie Wallace, early in his Mastership of the Heythrop in the 1950s.

After a good hunt *"they caught him close to the Toddington Church road. I was nearly beat as I struggled up the steep plough and they had just finished breaking up their fox as I reached them. Old Frantic as usual got the mask and will appear in the forefront of Mr Meads' picture carrying it in his mouth. Why do the 'Uglies' always put themselves in a conspicuous position?"*

At the end of the day *"the Fanshawes invited me in to tea and I picked up my car from the kennels, where I had left it this morning."*

However it was domestic problems that were to bring this successful Mastership to a premature end and no one was sadder than Daphne. Dick and Ruth Fanshawe split up and he handed in his resignation. Following a day's hunting from Mickleton at the end of December Daphne wrote: *"Called in to see Ruth on my way home. Dick is retiring from the Mastership and I cannot think WHAT is going to happen. It is such a tragic pity when all was going so swimmingly."*

In fact what happened was that Ruth Fanshawe became a Joint Master herself with the Hon. Anthony Wills, later to become Lord Dulverton and who she subsequently married, remaining Masters until 1959.

Daphne's income was now more and more dependent on what she could earn by her writing and she was also making a reputation for herself writing hound pedigrees for various Masters. During cubhunting in 1951,

on one such mission, she visited the Fitzwilliam (Milton). *"It came about through meeting Marcus Kimball at the Cottesmore Puppy Show in the summer, when Cyril Heber-Percy told him that I would write up their stud books, which have lapsed since 1936, and I fixed up to go and stay at the Milton kennels and sort things out once cubhunting began. So here I am, having driven up through considerable rain two days ago, reaching Marcus's house at the kennels in time for tea."*

Marcus Kimball later became a very influential Member of Parliament, who saw off many Bills that were designed to ban various field sports. He also became Chairman of the British Field Sports Society and the Cottesmore Hunt. However, he was now a young amateur huntsman, having cut his teeth with the Eton Beagles and the Cambridge University Drag. *"He has a wonderful zest for life and foxhunting, enjoys every moment of his Mastership, and is a perfect host."*

One of four Joint Masters (quite unusual in those days) he used to say he had *"taken a horn in a syndicate"*, but one of the Masters was of course Captain Tom Fitzwilliam, in whose family these hounds have been handed down from generation to generation for 200 years or more.

THE HUNTING SEASON...

OCTOBER 31st.   CROOME COURT.

(With the bitch pack.)

"And yet a little longer while, and glad November brings

With it the true commencement of the glorious "sport of Kings"—

The sport I've longed and waited for since last I trotted back,

In the dust of scentless April, from the blood-deserving pack."

(B.W. HICKS.)

Usually we are lucky in having a fine day for our Opening Meet, but this year the weather was against us & it simply poured with rain as hounds moved off from Croome. I was in a black mood of depression, for I had no horse to ride & it was the first Opening Meet for three years that I have been on my feet. Then I was nearly late, as I went with the Collie Morris's & they left their box at the Rhidings & I had to run nearly all the way across the Park, with the rain beating down in torrents so that I was soaked before I ever got there.

However, I did arrive in time, some 5 or 10 minutes before they moved off. There wasn't nearly such a big field as usual, on

CROOME MAKE A START

The **Croome** opening meet took place at Croome Court on Saturday, when heavy rain fell all the morning, with the result that the field was considerably smaller than usual. Hounds did not find until they reached Menagerie, where they disturbed a brace, killing their hunted fox in Pheasant Wood. Simultaneously a fox was holloa'd away from Boathouse covert and, hitting off the line, hounds crossed the river and road to Lickmore and the Old Park. Threading Pirton Gorse and Pool Covert, they ran over the road to Hermitage Farm, where scent, never good, failed altogether.

There were a brace in an old tree in the Park, one of which hounds ran in a right-handed circle through Salt Baths and over the river to the hunt stables, returning thence to the Park, where they lost him at the Oaks.

A typical example of a page in one of Daphne's hunting diaries, written in immaculate but tiny handwriting, with a drawing, a quote and a printed report.

On both cubhunting mornings the country was shrouded in fog and it was a case of waiting before moving off *"until the third telegraph pole was visible, which it never was."* However, on the second day, Daphne was mounted on a lovely old hunter owned by Marcus's mother.

"It was not long before they did get away from the fastness of Ashton Wold and we enjoyed a splendid forty-five minutes, negotiating some horrifying drains, as they call the open ditches, which ended successfully and I took home with me the brush. I am writing an article for Horse and Hound on this visit, as well as doing the Fitzwilliam Stud Books."

Daphne was now writing for both *The Field* and *Horse and Hound* on a regular basis, as was her old friend Bay de Courcy-Parry, who wrote under the name of 'Dalesman'. There are two particularly amusing correspondences, which were printed in *Horse and Hound* following articles written by Dalesman. In the first, he said, *"someone more literate than myself – perhaps Miss Daphne Moore, who can answer every "Hunting Quiz" without hesitation – will write to tell me who stated that only a huntsman knows a huntsman's cares. (I think it was Peter Beckford, but it does not matter, as it is very true and to the point.)"*

Daphne answered in the letter column,

"in answer to "Dalesman" it was, in fact, Mr Jorrocks (at the celebrated hunt dinner) who lamented the fact that "none but an 'untsman knows an 'untsman's cares."

Doubtless Mr Beckford felt it, though he never said so. It is the heart-cry of every huntsman from Nimrod down to the present day. But it is worth remembering Mr Jorrocks' subsequent words. "Care killed the cat!" he went on "Shan't kill me!" Heaven forbid that it should kill our friend "Dalesman" either!

Daphne Moore
Tewkesbury, Glos"

Dalesman replied:

"As our most versatile Miss Moore quoted in a recent issue, "Care killed the cat," but no one has ever given any reason why the cat died of such a complaint; to be modern one might say that "cats could not care less, and I feel certain than no cat feels that sense of responsibility that must continually rest upon the shoulders of a huntsman."

In another *Horse & Hound* article, Dalesman said; *"Of course Noah must have taken a couple of foxhounds with him into the Ark, and he must also have had a hard time amongst his stud books before*

The Puppy Show.

THEY were a lovely pack for looks . . .
Magpie and hare and badger-pie
Like minglings in a double dye.
Their flesh was sinew knit to bone,
Their courage like a banner blown.

JOHN MASEFIELD. 1919.

MAY 14th.

There was a very big entry of young hounds this year — no less than 27 couple all told, all but 2 couple being bitches, which made the classes for judging rather difficult. In the end all the bitches were judged together; the committee's with the rest, whilst the dogs had a small class of their own.

The judges this year were George Evans of the H.H. & Mr. Dalgety of the South Down. They arrived with George & Donne just before 11.30 (I had come by 'bus, so was at the kennels before them) together with Mrs. George Evans who is his joint-master.

John Masefield, one of Daphne's favourite poets, to whom she often referred in her diaries.

he decided which to select. No doubt our Daphne, who excels in these things, can trace a line or two back in all the best kennels, that is, to Noah's Ararat; above him will be written in her precise hand-writing and apparently done with a mapping pen, "All previous records lost in the Flood."

Daphne replied, again in the letter column:

"I am happy to inform our friend "Dalesman" that, far from the records having been lost in the Flood, we can, for a small consideration, trace his hounds'

137

genealogy back for a number of generations prior to the destruction of the Ark kennels. Mr Noah's Ararat, from whom most of the Babel hounds descend, goes back through Methusalah's Veteran to Cain's Carnage and Vengeance and Abel's Tragedy, to the celebrated Garden of Eden pack, showing lines to Adam's well-known Viper (B.C. 1,000,000) Tempter and Genesis.

Daphne Moore
Tewkesbury, Glos"

Daphne was now very prominent as a writer in the sporting press throughout the year, with a busy summer covering the hound shows, which could be why there seemed to be less time for otterhunting. 1950 was the last diary specifically for otterhunting, but the reason could be found in a small note she made early in that season: *"Ron signifies his intention of writing this season's reports, so I am giving up my job as Hawkstone Otterhounds' reporter – after 17 years!"*

CHAPTER ELEVEN

Hunting Tours

1951 was an important year for Daphne's writing career, as it saw the introduction of a weekly series in *Horse & Hound* entitled "Round the Kennels". This enabled her to visit kennels throughout the British Isles and Ireland.

In the autumn of that first year, following a couple of mornings' cubhunting with Ronnie Wallace at the Cotswold – they were the only pack able to start in mid-August that year – Daphne arrived at Dublin airport from Birmingham.

This was almost certainly the first time she had flown. She was met by the legendary Ikey Bell, an American, who as a Master both in Ireland and England, had more influence than almost anyone else on the development of the modern foxhound. Now elderly and severely crippled with arthritis, he had returned to Ireland to live at Ballyin, Lismore, one of the many properties of the Duke of Devonshire.

"After lunch at the Shelbourne, I drove with him and his nurse (for he is more or less an invalid now) to Lismore for the weekend.

Master of the Scarteen in Ireland from 1946 to 1986, Mr Thady Ryan, jumping a typical bank.

We drove through glorious country, but it was mainly obliterated by pouring rain which fell throughout; and reached Lismore during the evening, having talked 'hound' almost incessantly for some 90 miles."

Daphne later wrote in an article: "A recent sporting tour of Ireland revealed to me some of the finest hounds in existence. I saw the Carlow, Kilkenny, the inimitable Black-and-Tans, and many other long-established kennels and came home feeling that I had been in another world – a world in which time had stood still, a world far

removed from the bustle and rush of modern life, a world where kindness and hospitality are as natural as the air one breathes."

"The next day was fine and we motored over to Bonmahon to see the Waterford Hounds, which are kennelled at the home of the Master, Dick Russell, who is "Joint" with Lady Waterford. The Waterford have been, for generations, connected with the Beresford family and no fewer than four Marquesses of Waterford have been Masters. There were some nice hounds to be seen here, some not so nice. Ikey hadn't ever been to the kennels

NOVEMBER 1st. SUNDAY.

before and of course it was an education to me to hear his comments and see him judge individual hounds. In addition to the hounds, I shall always remember Dick Russell's home at Seafield for the exotic hydrangeas in every conceivable shade of heavenly blue, growing beside the drive."

The Scarteen are unique – firstly, the Ryan family have been Masters for

Mr Thady Ryan, pictured in 1962, with the famous 'Black and Tans', which have been hunted by a member of the Ryan family for over 350 years.

the last 300 years; and their hounds are the "Black and Tan" Kerry Beagles – though they are not, in fact, Beagles nor the Dumfriesshire type of black and tans, but stand 23 inches and hunt in their own characteristic style with a wonderful cry.

Daphne writes: *"I have for a very long time wanted to see the Scarteen (the great "Black & Tans"), and was more than delighted at Ikey's offer to take me there. And I wouldn't have missed this visit for worlds.*

Scarteen itself is typically Irish. The kennels lie at the back of the house, adjacent to the farmyard, and Thaddeus Ryan (generally known as Thady), sixth in succession as Master of the Black & Tans, showed us the hounds, and showed them beautifully. There are about 30 couple in kennel, every one of them black & tan except for the handsome "red" Admiral '49; Kerry Beagles do occasionally throw back to this coat-colour.

They were rather bigger than I expected. Their shoulders are perfect (Ikey describes them as like a cheetah's – probably the fastest animal in the world) and they have grand natural feet, which have never been known to let a toe down.

They are as hard as nails, with wonderful constitutions, and yet they must of necessity be fairly in-bred, as foxhound crosses have

not proved an unqualified success. Thady goes for an out-cross to the Kerry Beagle packs of the South West, which in turn possess much former Scarteen blood. I believe that their cry is remarkable and that Thady hunts them beautifully."

The following day it was to the Carlow, where Mrs Hall ('The Missus' to all in Ireland) had been Master for over thirty years; she retained that Mastership until she died in 1965. She was an unforgettable character, with a blunt, straightforward manner, and

Mrs Hall, long-time Master of the Carlow and universally known as 'The Missus'.

142

Sir Alfred Goodson MFH leading the College Valley field in their wild Northumbrian country in 1961.

could be extremely amusing, especially when she lapsed into the Irish brogue.

Daphne writes of her visit: *"it was a glorious drive over the mountains and the weather and visibility were perfect.*

We reached Mrs Hall's Kellistoon Cottage in time for lunch and drove to the kennels – only a stone's throw away – and I saw the hounds which seem to me the sort about which one dreams but so seldom sees. The bitches are superb; no words could ever exaggerate their quality. Their necks and

shoulders are perfect – and their appearance and bearing is so ALIVE and ALERT.

The highlight of a memorable day was when I found, whilst casually glancing through the names in the Puppy Book, under the 1928 entry – "Godfrey, sire Kilkenny Gory '21, dam, Carlow Goosecap '22." Foxhound history at close quarters!"

South & West Wilts Godfrey '28 was sent by Mrs Hall as a whelp to Ikey Bell, who entered him at the South & West Wilts, where he became probably

143

A photograph taken by Ikey Bell of Thady Ryan showing him and Daphne his famous Black and Tans at Scarteen on the occasion of their visit in 1951.

the most influential sire of the period between the wars. When Captain Brian Fanshawe was at the North Cotswold he was able to obtain two whelps of the best Carlow "ST" line, which were sent over by Captain Evan Williams, who was at the Tipperary at the time. This blood has now done untold good for very many English kennels.

From Lismore, Daphne moved on to stay with the Pigotts in Co Wicklow where she saw the Kilkenny hounds.

"We proceeded to the kennels at Mount Juliet with Victor McCalmont, where his father met us. He has been Master for 30 years, and now Victor has joined him and hunts hounds as his father did before him. The kennels were built by Major Dermot McCalmont when he took over the pack from Ikey Bell in 1921. They are model kennels, built on a very lavish scale, with a covered showing yard, which was lucky as the rain teemed down in torrents throughout.

One thing I particularly noticed about the Kilkenny was their strong muscular backs – a very hereditary trait I believe. There is a kind of cushion of muscle on either side of the spine, giving the appearance of a cloven back of immense strength. I do not remember noticing this so markedly in any other kennel. We spent so long looking at the hounds that there was no time to see the Stud Farm, where that great horse, The Tetrarch was bred.

Following the Carlow and the Kilkenny I found the Coollatin rather an anti-climax I'm afraid."

NOVEMBER 7th.   STONEBOW.
                                                 (With the mixed pack.)
"Oh, that weary scent! that weary, incomprehensible, incontrollable phenomenon!"

(MR. JORROCKS.)

144

One of the Masters, Lady Juliet Fitzwilliam, had become a Master at the age of 14 with her mother, following the death of her father, who had restarted the pack after the war. He was killed in a plane crash with his girlfriend, "Kick" Kennedy, sister of the future President of the United States, and by then the young widow of the Marquess of Hartington, the heir to Chatsworth.

"I think these hounds are coarse and shouldery – they lack quality – some "buckle-over" badly (an unforgivable sin in my eyes!). I saw them hunting in the big Coollatin Woods the next morning, 27½ couple of them, and thought they had a good

Huntsman of the Curre, Reg Dale, pictured in 1959 with some of the white Welsh-cross pack originally bred at Itton Court by Sir Edward Curre.

cry. *We left them early to see the Island in Kennel. These kennels lie close to Ferns, an historic village with a fine old ruined castle, and Two Bishop's Palaces! I believe this is a lovely unspoiled country to hunt over, but I do not like the hounds, which are great, coarse, bullock animals, and don't look as though they could gallop for more than ten yards without blowing up."*

The day before she was due to fly home, Daphne was dropped at the Kildare Kennels.

"The Fanshawes had given me an introduction to the Master – vast, bearded Michael Beamont, as rich as Croesus and with one of the most luxurious houses in Eire, to which I was invited for the night. I had not been expecting to like the Kildare from all I had heard of them, but I was pleasantly surprised, for the pedigrees are full of South & West Wilts Godfrey '28, Brecon Parragon '23 – through Bill Scott's Halo '34 – and Tedworth Plaintiff '27.

Founder, breeder and Master of the College Valley hounds from 1924 to 1979, Sir Alfred ('Bill') Goodson.

The kennels, incidentally, were built by Mr Eustace Loder in 1907, paid for with the money won by his celebrated mare, Pretty Polly. Thus ended a memorable visit to this incomparable island."

Daphne was a close friend of Bridget Scott, Bill Scott's first wife, and at that time a Master of the Hursley. For some time they had planned a trip to Wales and in October they set off for a day with the Curre. These hounds, bred by Sir Edward Curre during his Mastership from 1896 to his death in 1930 (when Lady Curre took over until 1956), probably had more influence on the development of the modern foxhound, as we know it today, than any others.

It was to Sir Edward that many great hound breeders, such as Ikey Bell, went at that time to get the best of the Welsh blood that had already been successfully crossed with the English. The Curre country itself is a relatively small and rough one in south-east Monmouthshire and, as Daphne says:

"strictly speaking, of course, Monmouthshire is not in Wales at all yet when the meet is held at a place called Nant-y-Gelli this is hard indeed to comprehend. More Welsh than English too, were the deep-wooded dingles and bracken-covered hills; whilst it was from Welsh ancestors

of half a century ago that were derived the rough and broken coats of some of the hounds — that famous white pack bred for so long and so brilliantly by the late Sir Edward Curre. Reg Dale hunted hounds and, curiously enough, none of the young hounds were out; we did not like to ask the reason. It was trying to rain and later settled down into a Welsh downpour, so we took the car down a lane and watched from a distance. There was little scent and, not until some while later, when they were drawing some really big woodlands, did we hear the Welsh chorus we had hoped for.

We were also most disappointed in the hounds — so many bad feet and shoulders. The current Master, Mr & Mrs Meade are tremendously keen and so anxious to improve the pack. I am afraid they cannot hope to be the same as in Sir Edward's day, but without that Master-Mind it would be impossible."

Daphne and Bridget Scott now set off West to the Carmarthenshire country; where Lt. Col. W.H. Buckley had been Master since 1931, when he took over from Lord Coventry, and he remained Master until 1964. "Billy" Buckley was an old friend of Daphne's and had inherited a wonderful pack of Welsh-cross hounds from George Coventry.

Unfortunately, the pack was disbanded while the Master was abroad throughout the war, with a nucleus being put out to walk on local farms. Sadly Daphne did not find the quality pack of pre-war days. *"After a very wet journey to Castell Gorfod, we arrived in time for tea, but even before tea Billy insisted on me going out to see hounds "wetly" in their improved kennels. These have been built on to and made much more workable, but today they seemed very primitive to me, and extremely smelly!*

As with the Curre, I was bitterly disappointed in the hounds. They have certainly gone wrong somewhere, but there is no doubt that they have lost their lovely shoulders, have poor feet and there are very few I would want to take home with me. There are just a few which George Coventry might have bred – Leisure and Levity '56, by College Valley Legion and a few more which could be counted on the fingers of one hand. There are some enormous rough tan dogs, and some English-y types of the worst kind.

I could have cried. It is Billy's intention to present Master with a bitch, but really I can't see any of these proving acceptable, which is most awkward, since I was deputed to choose one. Fred James, who came here in 1931 and has hunted hounds for the past seven seasons, is very ill with Thrombosis, so Billy has it all to do and is also hunting hounds himself again after an interim of years.

The morning's cubhunting is difficult to describe. We hunted the hills around Castell Gorfod and galloped about from one side of the valley to the other, but somehow the whole thing was Bedlam! Billy had a horn, George Evans (his amateur whipper-in) had a horn, and there seemed little rhyme or reason in anything. In the end a fox was alleged to have gone to ground in a vast bramble patch on the open hillside and was left."

Lt. Colonel 'Bill' Buckley, Master of the Carmarthenshire Foxhounds from 1931 to 1964 and longstanding friend of Daphne's, taken at Castell Gorfod in 1962.

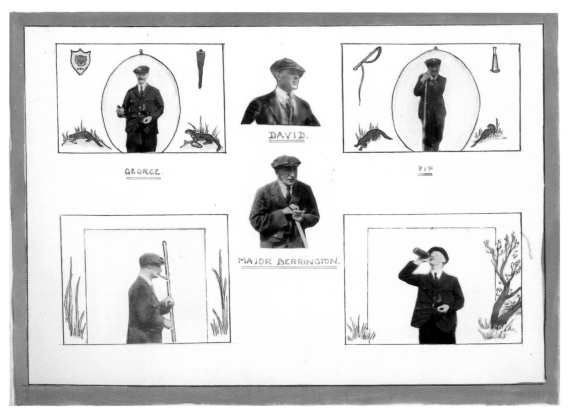

Daphne was rather fond of creating these colourful montages of her hunting friends, hand-tinting newspaper cuttings.

However, there were no such criticisms in Daphne's article for *Horse & Hound* in which she expounds on the various breeding lines in the kennel and even chose the aforementioned 'Leisure' to go to Badminton.

"A recent infusion of College Valley blood has proved a success at Castell Gorfod, where a broken coated litter out of Sidelamp '56, has since been given to the Duke of Beaufort, and has acquitted herself most creditably, hunting with the flying Badminton bitch-pack."

The next step was to see the South Pembrokeshire in kennels. Pembrokeshire, as a country, is always known as "England beyond Wales", and the hounds are also English bred.

"We spent the afternoon seeing the South Pembrokeshire in kennel. They are pretty level, very well turned out, very "orthodox", and well shown and the Hunt

Sir Alfred Goodson pictured with his unique pack of Fell-cross hounds, the College Valley, which he bred with a devastating ability to kill a large number of their hunted foxes.

Staff and whole set-up is extremely smart. To me it was of the greatest interest to see the Grande Dame, the Duke of Beaufort's Ribbon '50, litter sister to the Peterborough Champion, Ringbolt, still full of life and the dam of no fewer than 22 hounds now in kennel, to say nothing of numerous grandchildren."

These hounds have been, for the great part of their history, in the hands of the Allen family at Cresselly since the 18th century. Hugh Harrison-Allen is Master today and his ancestor, Mr Seymour Allen, who was a Master from 1893 to 1929, was a legendary figure who had a rope suspended from the high ceiling above the staircase, which he climbed nightly on his way to bed with the object of retaining his fitness. The hook from which the rope was hung remains to this day.

A week later, having had a day with the Berkeley and another with the Beaufort bitches, Daphne and Bridget Scott embarked on a Northern Tour.

"Setting off from Badminton station two days ago, I met Bridget Scott in London. I look upon the capital with a mixture of awe and terror. My sole consolation was the fleeting view of a magnificent bronze foxhound standing at the entrance to the Kennel Club past which my intrepid taxi driver was piloting his vehicle like a veritable Jehu. We proceeded together by British Railways to Harrogate.

It was an appalling journey, with derailments and delays all the way. The first pack to be seen was the Zetland in North Yorkshire where the hounds looked delightfully fit, stripped right down and in real hunting condition. It was interesting, in view of my recent visit to the South Pembrokeshire, where the Duke of Beaufort's Ribbon '50 had virtually "bred the pack", to find at the Zetland kennels the strong influence of her brother, Ringbold '50, Peterborough Champion of 1952, who was lent to Capt MacAndrew in 1955. The Master also swears by the blood of Critic '51, who came from the Warwickshire unentered and bred a high percentage of good working hounds."

Colin MacAndrew, later Lord MacAndrew, was Master and huntsman of the Zetland from 1949 to 1965 and was one of the top amateur huntsmen of his day.

"And so on to our "pied a terre", the Blue Bell at Belford in Northumberland from where we hunted with the College Valley. Many, many years earlier before the war, I had heard of the College Valley when George Coventry spoke of this wonderful pack of cross-bred Fell-English hounds, established by Sir Alfred Goodson in 1924 and maintained by him ever since. Light coated, many of them pure white, these hounds are all quality, built for speed.

This morning's meet was not very far away, and upon those high hills the air was like champagne and the almost cloudless blue sky was reflected in the little College burn, from

The distinctive black and tan hounds of the Dumfriesshire Foxhounds in their kennels near Lockerbie.

Sir John Buchanan-Jardine with some of his unique Dumfriesshire Foxhounds – the result of his great skill as a breeder and extensive knowledge of genetics.

which the hunt takes its name. Bill Goodson is such a splendid chap and hunting with him is a happy, light hearted affair.

During the course of the morning he came past us giving a lively rendering of "John Peel" on his hunting horn, for our benefit! There were 16 couple of hounds and they hunted continuously with a grand cry, and with great drive, despite very indifferent scent. There was scarcely a moment when they were not busily hunting or casting themselves at a check. I saw them once climbing a seemingly perpendicular rock face, emphasising the necessity for the faultless feet which are such a characteristic of this kennel.

Another noteworthy point is the longevity of the hounds, despite the hard conditions under which they hunt. Balance between nose and drive is always carefully considered by the Master, for too much of one or too *little of the other would be a grave fault in a pack which so largely hunts itself. Sir Alfred has long been known as an expert breeder of livestock, and he brought his expertise into full use when it came to breeding foxhounds. This evening the Goodsons gave us a grand Foxhunters' dinner at the Blue Bell and the Master of the Milvain, Mr Jeffreys, and his wife, were in the party.*

The following morning was spent in the Milvain kennels – the hounds in the Chapel – whose unique kennels were really more interesting than the hounds themselves. These were formerly Col. Milvain's and only about 1½ couple remain of these – "orthodox" hounds of the worst type. The present Master, Mr Dick Jeffreys, is now building up a pack largely on College Valley blood, but these have not so far had the time to become anything very impressive. However, I would have liked to have seen them hunt.

We then lunched with the Goodsons at Kilham and spent the afternoon seeing the College Valley shown to us by their Master and huntsman. How he loves them! And no wonder. As well as being a wonderful and unique pack, they have such individual charm."

The next pack to be seen was the Dumfriesshire, whose hounds were quite unique, and there was no other pack of hounds of their type in the world. Tragically, they were disbanded at the time of the Hunting Act in 2005 and, although restarted a few years later, the original pack, as such, had been lost. They were the result of the lifework of Sir John Buchanan-Jardine, who became Master on his coming-of-age in 1921. The Dumfriesshire hounds are all dark black and tan, standing nearly 28 inches at the shoulder, with deep booming voices.

The new Master, starting from scratch, bred for the characteristics that he cherished above all other, of cry and colour. He wanted a pack of pure black and tans, with a much better cry than the orthodox foxhound, as well as speed and nose.

He brought his extensive knowledge of genetics to bear on the breeding of his hounds, choosing as his foundation bitches the daughters of a stud book dog with a very superior nose and tongue, Dumfriesshire Fireman '28. He mated these bitches with a French sire of Gascon-Santongeois blood, called Triomphe.

The combination of these two strains produced the tongue for which he was striving, and the nose was improved by the use of a bloodhound. He continued to experiment with French blood and also several orthodox

Daphne's watercolour illustrations would often be painted on the lined paper of her written diary.

black-and-tan doghounds. He had worked out that genetically a "whole" colour would be dominant to a part colour and therefore, by always using whole-coloured doghounds, he would eventually eliminate the white. Croome Clausman '34, bred of course by George Coventry, was one such dog that proved a successful "nick".

Daphne describes the cry of this pack as *"something quite out of this world. It might be likened to the music of an organ with all the stops out; each individual hound possessing a deep bass voice – doghounds and bitches alike – and each hound "held" its note like a singer, so that the concerted cry had to be heard to be believed."*

On the morning in question, the hunted fox *"passed so close that I could almost count his whiskers! The cry of the pack as a whole was nothing less than terrifying, but I think they are very* *headstrong and will flash on over the line and take some getting back."*

Hounds were being hunted at this time by Sir John's son, Rupert, who Daphne noted showed excellent "houndmanship" in going to fetch them at the next check, when the fox had been headed.

"I believe these hounds need different handling from the ordinary foxhound. They are not foxhounds in the ordinary sense; they are bloodhounds, staghound, foxhound and must possess characteristics of each." But, as Daphne remembers, *"when the pack came sweeping past me in a great tidal-wave of black-and-tan, with a resounding roar which almost shook the trees; it was something to be recalled in dreams."*

A further visit was to Dorset to see the American former Master of both the Cattistock and South Dorset, Henry Higginson. He had been

154

Master of several packs of hounds in the United States and had been President of the MFHA of America for seventeen years. He was a talented and entertaining author, writing many books about hunting on both sides of the Atlantic. "Hig", as he came to be known, was a popular and successful Master, always a showman and never losing his strong American accent. His wife was the well known West End actress, Mary Newcombe.

He had written to Daphne, suggesting that she came to stay – *"Just name your weekend and let me know what day to expect you. I'm delighted at the idea of meeting you after so many years of postal acquaintance."*

Daphne had a wonderful weekend. *"Mr Higginson is a charming old man and his house is absolutely perfect. The atmosphere simple breathes hunting. There is hardly a square inch of wall not covered with pictures of horses or hounds. The library is a dream; it contains all my favourite sporting books, all the books on hunting I have ever wanted to read, a great many I have never heard of, all the classics on sport, an original edition of Peter Beckford. I longed for more time to read them.*

At dinner he summons his brother with a blast upon a lovely chased silver presentation hunting horn, which was owned by the famous Jem Tredwell, Mr Farqharson's huntsman in 1858. We talked 'hound talk' solemnly until bed-time."

The following day Daphne writes, *"I have reckoned out that my host and I have today talked for nearly 10 hours! This is a foxhunter's paradise. Mr Higginson and I breakfasted in our respective rooms and met at about 10 o'c to look at pictures, photographs, books and diaries (he is the most wonderful diarist) – and to talk! We walked round the garden, ate peaches off the wall, saw the hunters out at grass, and got back to lunch at 1.0'c, still talking!*

After tea we went down to the cellars – where there are masses more pictures and no room for them! – and saw a most interesting oil-painting, simply enormous, of Peter Beckford's hounds. It was rescued from an old barn and Mr Higginson had it cleaned and restored. Mr Higginson owned a good many steeplechasers in America and rode many of them himself. He is also a keen fisherman and altogether he is quite one of the most interesting people I have ever met."

There can have been very few people at that time who had visited so many hunting countries and had the depth of knowledge of the hounds in the kennels, the Masters who had bred them and the Hunt Servants who had handled them. Daphne Moore was already unique in the world of hunting.

April 26th. Sunday.

CHAPTER TWELVE

Hounds and Shows

Daphne Moore was at the centre of the exciting new developments in hound breeding. Before the war, George Coventry was one of the Masters who were not happy with the type of hound prevailing at the time.

He and others found encouragement and advice from Mr Isaac (Ikey) Bell, who became firm friends with Daphne in later years. He had moved from Ireland in the 1920s to hunt the South and West Wilts hounds.

Ikey Bell was an American with no hunting background, but he was rich, highly intelligent and with boundless enthusiasm for hounds and hunting. He was convinced that the answer to these problems lay in Wales and that by crossing their hounds with the Welsh foxhound these Masters would obtain the activity, intelligence, nose and tongue that they were looking for.

These forward-looking English Masters went to four Welsh hound

Captain Ronnie Wallace and his wife Rosie at Peterborough Royal Foxhound Show in 1964 having just won the Doghound Championship with the unentered Heythrop Cardinal. They are flanked by the two senior judges, both Masters in Ireland, Major Victor McCalmont (Kilkenny), who judged the doghounds, and Captain Evan Williams (Tipperary), who judged the bitches.

breeders who had already bred outstanding packs by crossing the best of the English lines with their native Welsh hounds. They were Sir Edward Curre of Itton; Mr Jack Evans, Master of the Brecon; Mr David Davies, who hunted his own private pack; and of course Lord Coventry, while he was still at the Carmarthen.

Great bitterness was caused by this use of Welsh blood and many of the old guard believed that it was the ruination of the foxhound. Ikey Bell was accused of being a menace to the foxhound –

158

he replied that he would prefer to be remembered as a menace to foxes!

Feelings continued to run high, especially when "Master", the 10th Duke of Beaufort, successfully introduced the new blood into his kennel by using Tiverton Actor '22 and some of Ikey Bell's best lines. Lord Bathurst, a major opponent, described the Welsh-cross as *"a blot on the escutcheon, a mésalliance, a marriage without quarterings."*

Even in the late 1800s, N. Cumberland Bentley wrote a delightful poem about a Welsh-cross bitch that was sent from Wales to the Pytchley:

But see! The pack are scattered;
*   for baffled by the stain*
Left by the herded cattle, they seek the line
*   in vain.*
Hark! There's a distant holloa, and down
*   the highway there*
That sandy bitch has got it
*   – she's right again I swear!*

Fast fly the golden minutes, yet all
*   throughout the run*
The sandy bitch cuts out the work,
*   and shows them all the fun;*
She's there from find to finish;
*   she leads from first to last*
Until "who-oop!" it's over;
*   the gallop's done and past.*

And now all ask in vain what hound it
*   was that did so well;*
Both whips are questioned, but don't
*   know, or if they do, won't tell.*
"Where did she come from? What's her
*   name? Come, Goodall, won't you say?"*
"It's Dimple", Goodall says at last,
*   and turning rides away.*

Those verses show that even that great huntsman Will Goodall did not care, at that time, for his experiment to be voiced abroad!

The poem continues until it is noticed in the New Year that Dimple is no longer at the meet.

Tis then we learn her pedigree,
*   and what her dam and sire;*

From Wales, Lort-Phillips sent her down
*   to fair Northamptonshire.*

He sent her there to test her nose,
*   her courage and her speed,*

And seek comparison with hounds of
*   the famed Pytchley breed.*

No more her melody we'll hear,
*   no more she'll lead the pack*

Until they break from scent to view,
*   for Dimple has gone back.*

Dimple – Llangibby Danger sire; her dam
*   from Taunton Vale –*

No more will be our pilot over Pytchley hill
*   and dale.*

When that great amateur huntsman, Mr Charles McNeill, became Master of the Grafton in 1907, he took over a fairly moderate pack. He asked the hound committee if they wished him to breed a 'Peterborough' kennel, or one of smashing workers – he could not guarantee to do both. Needless to say, they asked him for the latter!

One of the first hounds that he added to the pack was Sir Edward Curre's Globule '03. Many a fox in those dense woodlands owed his doom to Globule, and every follower soon knew his note.

The Duke of Beaufort's great friend, Sir Peter Farquhar, was a firm advocate of the Welsh-cross during his Masterships of the Whaddon Chase and the Meynell.

After the war, Sir Peter moved to the Portman and, during the twelve years of his Mastership there, with his Joint Master Bill Scott, produced some

Pictured at the 'unique hound-showing event', held in 1955, where five former champions were judged at the Heythrop kennels, are three of the Masters involved: Mr Percival Williams (Four Burrow), the Duke of Beaufort (his own), and Lord Irwin, later to become Lord Middleton (Middleton).

The class for Two Couple of Entered Bitches being judged at Peterborough in 2014 by the author of this book, Mr Alastair Jackson, and Mr Andrew Sallis, Master of the East Sussex and Romney Marsh.

of the most influential stallion hounds of modern times. A young man at the time who took full advantage of those stallion hounds was Captain Ronnie Wallace, starting his 25-year Mastership of the Heythrop.

These were all men who Daphne knew well. She visited all their kennels, listened to their hound talk, and followed their hounds in the field. Through her writing and deep knowledge, she became the advocate for the modern foxhound.

During his third year at the Heythrop, Ronnie Wallace produced Harper '53, by Sir Peter's Portman Lovelock '47, to win the championship at Peterborough, and for the next quarter of a century the Beaufort and the Heythrop were the main influence on hound breeding. Year after year Daphne Moore wrote in *Horse & Hound* on the "battle of the green coats" at the major hound shows.

Peterborough Show is the "shop window" for the foxhound and is the senior of the five regional shows held at Harrogate in the north, Ardingly in the south, Honiton in the west and Builth Wells in Wales. It is more formal than the other shows with, until recently, all gentlemen wearing bowler hats, stiff white collars and carrying umbrellas, with smart dresses and hats for the ladies. It is only the Peterborough Dog and Bitch champions that have their

Daphne Moore, typically dressed for a day foot following, with the Duke of Beaufort's bitch pack in 1973.

photographs in the annual Foxhound Kennel Studbook, showing the standard of their times.

Daphne Moore, as doyenne of Peterborough correspondents for *Horse and Hound* for over forty years, wrote: *"There is a certain atmosphere, almost ecclesiastical, which pervades the ring at Peterborough, which might well be called the Temple of the Foxhound."*

She continues in her *Book of the Foxhound*: *"Peterborough is the Foxhunter's Mecca, and every MFH should attend if at all possible. It has been said that there are many imitators, but only one Peterborough, and Peterborough of course stands head and shoulders above the various other Hound Shows, excellent through these may be. Here devotees come from far and wide, from overseas (frequently American visitors attend, though only one American has ever*

The two Peterborough Champions in 1978. (left) The Duke of Beaufort's Monmouth '77, the first recent Welsh-cross doghound to win such honours, and (right) Kilkenny Famous '77, Bitch Champion, who had come over from Ireland, bred by Major Victor McCalmont. The Prince of Wales was President of the show that year and watched most of the judging.

judged at Peterborough, the late Mr. A. H. Higginson in 1946), from Ireland, Scotland and from Wales."

Since then, Mr. C. Martin Wood, Master of his own hounds, the Live Oak in Georgia, USA, judged in 2001.

Most people recognized that, in later life, Daphne could be somewhat over-partisan in support of most Badminton hounds and some of her reports were full of their glowing descriptions. Writing in her diary of the 1952 Peterborough show, she noted:

"This year was very good indeed, and the bitches were of higher standard than for many a long day – whilst the doghounds were about the best I have ever seen – Master's lovely Ringbolt '50 is unbeatable and of course won the doghound championship, but only he could have beaten Portman Playfair '51. He really is the most glorious dog; standing still you can never catch him wrong, whilst when he moves – it is the very poetry of motion."

A few weeks later at Honiton, she wrote *"Master won both championships! Of course, the doghound championship was a foregone conclusion, for nothing, I believe, not even a hound from the golden benches of St. Hubert's kennel, could ever beat Ringbolt."*

However, probably the most memorable year for Daphne, amongst her Peterborough reports for *Horse & Hound*, would have been many years later in 1978, for several reasons.

Firstly it was the centenary show; secondly the President was H.R.H. the Prince of Wales; and thirdly the champion doghound was the Duke of Beaufort's Monmouth '77, the first recent Welsh-cross doghound to win such honours. Monmouth was by Sir Newton Rycroft's influential rough-coated stallion hound New Forest Medyg '69, who was in turn by the pure Welsh dog Plas Machynlleth Miller '63.

Describing the champion, Daphne says: *"His clean-cut lines, fit and hard appearance – not an ounce of superfluous flesh – lovely neck and shoulder, muscular hind leg and low-set hocks combine in a charming whole. But a foxhound is not designed to stand still, and with his speedy build he galloped to victory to make history as the pioneer Peterborough champion of*

Lt. Col. Sir Peter Farquhar hunting the Portman hounds in the 1950s.

second-cross *Welsh breeding. It was a notable victory and one that will be long remembered as setting the seal upon the new judiciously blended, Welsh-cross. And how many, I wonder, of the ringside spectators realised the significance of Monmouth's win?"*

Explaining why that year's centenary show was so remarkable, she writes: *"First and foremost, H.R.H. the Prince of Wales was president, making the occasion a right Royal one, and making history in that he followed his great-great-grandfather, King Edward VII, who as Prince of Wales conferred a similar honour in 1895, and, more recently, the Prince of Wales, later the Duke of Windsor, in 1923.*

It is gratifying indeed that Prince Charles possesses such a genuine interest in the foxhound that he was present during the greater part of the judging, intent upon all that occurred in the ring."

It is interesting to note that the bitch championship was won that year by Kilkenny Famous '77, who had come over from Ireland, bred by Major Victor McCalmont.

Daphne attended an increasing number of Puppy Shows – where the young hounds from a Hunt, which are due to start hunting in the autumn, are judged for conformation and prizes

The brilliant – if somewhat unorthodox – hound breeder, Sir Newton Rycroft, hunting the New Forest Foxhounds, pictured with his Joint Master, Mrs Bridget Scott, former wife of the celebrated Master, Major Bill Scott, and a great friend of Daphne's.

given to the puppy walkers, who have had them at their homes for several months as part of the young hounds' education. The Puppy Shows for the larger hunts would also be attended by visiting Masters and hunt staff and Daphne often wrote reports for *Horse & Hound*. The first Puppy Show that she actually judged herself was that of the West Warwickshire Farmers in 1955.

In her diary she writes: *"Although I boggled at the idea of making a speech, I agreed to help to judge with Ralph Perry, the Croome Huntsman. There was only a very small entry, and the doghounds frankly horrors. One couple had perpendicular shoulders, another couple were so flat-sided that it was "like looking at a penny sideways" as old Reg Blizard used to say... and the rest had shocking sterns.*

Perry whispered to me early on — *"What are we going to do about those sterns, Miss?"* and in the end we decided them to be the lesser evil, though it went against the grain to perpetuate this defect by awarding the puppy walkers a prize!"

A couple of weeks later, Daphne was asked to judge the Hampshire Hunt Puppy Show.

"Master was originally invited to judge; when he couldn't do so, I was substituted, so

felt very honoured! I drove down from Badminton where I have been looking after the dogs this week, Master and Mary staying with the Queen at Windsor since it is Ascot week."

Writing up the show in *Horse & Hound*, Daphne started her article by saying: *"Judging a young entry, whether*

The winner of the 'unique hound-showing event', held at the Heythrop kennels in 1955, Duke of Beaufort's Distaff '52, shown by kennel-huntsman, Bert Pateman.

Captain Ronnie Wallace was Master of the Exmoor Foxhounds from 1977 until his death in 2002.

officially or from the ringside, is undoubtedly one of the pleasantest occupations of the so-called Idle Summer. And when the entry is excellent, the hounds beautifully shown and the weather perfect, what more could be desired?"

There was dismay, though, when it came to the Berkeley Puppy Show.

"It was a great disappointment about today. At Master's Puppy Show, Brian Bell told me that I was being invited to judge the Berkeley entry. I was delighted, but grew anxious when I heard nothing further and eventually my ordinary invitation arrived and I gave up hope! It appears that Rob Berkeley, after having, presumably, suggested me, went off and invited Ronnie to judge with Master. It was a bitter thing for me, as to judge with Master would have been an education."

A unique hound-showing event took place at the end of the summer season of 1955. Following Honiton Show, when the Peterborough Champion, Heythrop Harper '53, was beaten by a doghound from the South Hereford, it was decided to have a private show at the Heythrop kennels to judge the supreme champion doghound from a number of champions of that year.

"Consequent upon the championship at Honiton, where the S. Hereford dog, Merchant '52, beat the Heythrop champion Peterborough dog, Harper '53, a private hound show was arranged by Master and Ronnie with independent judges – Mo

Barclay and Peach Borwick – to decide the respective merits of Merchant and Harper, and, in addition, Master's Distaff '52 and Middleton and Four Burrow dogs.

The judges took a great deal of time and trouble over the final decision, between Distaff and Harper, and eventually did the right thing in giving supreme championship to the former, which had been Peterborough champion the previous year. But Ronnie didn't mind being beaten by him – it was the South Hereford dog which rankled, and

Daphne Moore at a meet of the Beaufort in 1973 with professional huntsman, Brian Gupwell.

he was discarded, together with the horrible Four Burrow Major, and the rather nice Middleton dog, who was unfortunately too lame to show himself to any advantage. Though a private function, there was an enormous crowd, including Mrs Hall from the Carlow, and the Farquhars. Tea was provided in a marquee and there must have been about 100 people present."

It was a rather different sort of day when Daphne was asked to judge the Welsh Hound Association Show at Carmarthen in 1960.

"I was not informed until quite recently that I was to judge alone. I protested, but all to no avail, and my apprehensions were more than justified! The Hound Show was held in a dimly lit marquee. Billy Buckley was my ring steward; he had forgotten his spectacles and could not see to read the catalogue and in the dim light and without glasses I could not do so either – so the blind

was quite literally leading the blind! Hounds were on grass except for a small central board which cracked with the combined weight of man and hound, leaving large jagged holes, and, as always at Welsh shows, hounds were dragged round on couples and one couldn't see them move."

Although her *Horse and Hound* report does not say so, in her diary Daphne comments on the *"bad feet, straight shoulders, terrible backs, and I think the current Welsh hound is a deplorable animal – and almost impossible to judge under the conditions of a Welsh Hound Show as constituted."*

It would be true to say that the standards of the current Welsh hounds have been improved out of all recognition and restored to their pre-war excellence.

CHAPTER THIRTEEN

Hunting Through the '50s and the move to Badminton

To Daphne's delight, Dick Fanshawe had been called out of retirement in 1954 to hunt the North Cotswold as amateur huntsman.

"They have had several successful mornings so far with Dicky as huntsman, Albert having departed to the Whaddon Chase. Ruth continues as Master with Tony Wills – an ideal partnership."

At the Beaufort the long serving Hunt Secretary, Major Gerald Gundry, became a Joint Master in 1951 and hunted the doghounds himself on Mondays and Thursdays. The Duke described him as *"my Joint Master and more than my right arm."*

In Daphne's eyes, however, no-one could be compared to Master as a huntsman and she was perhaps somewhat unfairly critical of Gerald Gundry when hunting hounds. Cubhunting in September 1954, she writes, *"I have heard many stories of the wildness of Gerald's doghounds and only half believed them, but was horrified today at their behaviour which was terribly undisciplined. On reaching the first covert – where Master and I placed ourselves at a* strategic point – *hounds began to race round with a great cry and I thought they had found immediately, but it was merely exuberance of spirits and the covert was blank."*

At the end of the morning Daphne returned to Badminton, where, *"after lunch Mary's Rabbit Hounds and several visiting dogs were hunted by young Anthony Brassey, whipped-in to by Master Morgan-Jones, killing 3 rabbits in the*

Major Gerald Gundry, Joint Master with the Duke of Beaufort, on a day he was acting as Field Master, with his wife Ferelith.

Pleasure Grounds before I left. They appear to be rather more successful than Gerald's doghounds!"

A much younger amateur huntsman, who would later make a great name for himself, was also starting his career.

"This season young Anthony Hart, who is only 21 this year, has taken over the Mastership of the Cotswold Vale Farmers – extremely courageous, probably very foolhardy, but he has tremendous self-confidence, and I think that he may well make a success of it.

The hounds are appalling, but both Master and Ronnie have given him hounds, entered and unentered, so he starts off on the right leg. Rather misguidedly, I feel, he has kept on Sam Wright as kennel-huntsman. As he was sacked from the Berkeley for being drunk in charge of hounds and as the C.V.F is notorious for pub-crawling, it seems a pity to retain his services. I bicycled to the meet

Major Bill Scott hunting with the Heythrop at the time that he took over as 'deputy huntsman' when Ronnie Wallace was injured. Probably the only occasion that the Heythrop, whose livery is green, have been hunted by someone wearing a red coat.

NOVEMBER 7TH. SATURDAY.   OPENING MEET.

"And oh! if there be an elysium on earth,

It is this. It is this"

THOMAS MOORE.

Ronnie Wallace pictured with Lt. Colonel Raymond Barrow, who, on the insistence of the Hunt committee, was his Joint Master on his arrival at the Heythrop.

this morning, arriving just in time. Norman Hart (Anthony's father) was out in his car, having come from home and brought Chris (Anthony's brother), who was whipping-in to Anthony in Sam's absence on holiday.

I thought it was a wonderful gesture on Anthony's part to make a start when his K.H. is away, in order to show that he is not indispensable!

Chris made a most efficient whipper-in. He is Master of the Radley Beagles this

time, so must be about 17, but he looks far younger and was nearly swallowed up in Anthony's "second best" red coat which practically enveloped him from top to toe!"

After a busy morning, "a cub was subsequently found in a small roadside covert near Apperley and not far from the river. Hounds very soon accounted for him and Anthony was well satisfied to call them out for home."

Meanwhile, Daphne was doing more and more pedigree work. *"I came down to Turnworth yesterday to discuss with Peter (Sir Peter Farquhar) the pedigree book I am doing for him, commissioned by Ikey."*

She had also been called in by the Editor of the *Foxhound Kennel Stud Book* himself.

"I have for months been going to stay at John Chamberlayne's in order to help him with the F.K.S.B. entries and this weekend was finally decided upon so that I could kill two birds with one stone and attend the Heythrop Opening Meet – my third this week."

Ronnie Wallace had moved from the Cotswold in 1952 as Joint Master and huntsman of the Heythrop. There had been opposition to this move amongst some at the Heythrop and it seems unbelievable in hindsight, after his legendary twenty-five year Mastership here, that he was only accepted with a majority of one – and this on the understanding that his Joint Master would be the Lt.Col. Raymond Barrow, a well-respected Heythrop landowner.

The objections seemed to be that the Heythrop had always employed a professional huntsman and that Percy Durno had hunted hounds here very satisfactorily for fourteen years; that Ronnie's startling success at the Cotswold could not have been achieved without "cheating" in some way; they did not approve of his marital arrangements; and that, having managed to hunt hounds during some of the wartime years, he had somehow had a "bad war".

However, the doubters were very soon proved wrong and the Heythrop country still reaps the rewards of Ronnie Wallace's remarkable dedication and organisational ability. During his Mastership, nothing was "left to chance" – from the sale of farms and letting of shoots to the earthstopping and fencing – and coupled with a remarkable natural talent as a huntsman and hound breeder, the result was a

sustained period of sport probably unequalled anywhere for that length of time and at that standard.

Daphne now hunted as often as she could with the Heythrop. She had of course known Ronnie Wallace since he was a schoolboy, had whipped-in to him when he hunted the Eton College Beagles and followed him as a Master and huntsman of the Hawkstone otterhounds.

"The faithful and incomparable Percy Durno", former huntsman of the Heythrop and then an immensely popular and loyal kennel-huntsman and 1st whipper-in to Ronnie Wallace.

"I was out as often as possible with this outstanding pack of foxhounds in what I have heard described as "the best country in England". The influence of the Heythrop blood cannot be exaggerated; it has spread to almost every kennel throughout the foxhunting world and has proved an immense influence for good. To relate in detail the brilliant sport which – even on foot – I witnessed with the Heythrop during the 1950s, would fill a volume."

Following a day from Fox Farm in January 1957 Daphne found herself the object of Ronnie's fury, having inadvertently headed his fox and hidden herself to avoid doing so.

"To my horror Ronnie was rapidly approaching me, hounds had checked, and quite obviously I had badly headed his fox. He demanded of me WHERE THE FOX HAD GONE? And I had no choice but to say that, as I was hiding I was unable to see, to which he replied that I should keep my eye on the fox to see which way he went – but how could I when I was doing everything in my power not to be seen?

When I came up with them again, I hid myself among the horses. Ronnie, of course, viewed me and opened fire again, completing the barrage by saying that what I had really been doing was trying to hide from HIM, not the fox! All of which delighted the field who were within earshot!"

Daphne Moore foot following on a spring day in the hills, pictured with Beaufort Hunt secretary, Major Ronnie Dallas.

The diary note ends with an N.B. *"Ronnie was evidently stricken by remorse when he got home, and sent me a copy of his current hound-list with notes on the loan of his various stallion hounds to kennels far and wide, as follows:*

CHIEFTAIN '50 to Limerick, FEUDAL '53 to West Dulverton, HARPER '53 to Fitzwilliam, CRACKER '54 to Kilkenny, PALAFOX '55 to Carlow, PAINTER '55 to Berwickshire… Also a very nice note, hoping to see me out again soon!"

Daphne had been to five Opening Meets in 1955 and at the Heythrop *"the faithful and incomparable Percy Durno was badly concussed and was sent home.*

Her Majesty the Queen broke her journey between Banbury and Chipping Norton to meet Ronnie Wallace and the Heythrop hounds in 1957.

His horse apparently jumped very big and jumped him into a tree, hitting his head."

He was still not able to go hunting when hounds met at Donnington two weeks later. The second whipper-in, Sidney Bailey, the kennelman's son, later to become the longtime and very well respected huntsman of the VWH, was whipping in, with some help from Major Bill Scott, who had retired from the Mastership of the Portman and was now living on the Heythrop-Cotswold border.

"A disastrous day, though we had a good hunt to finish with, but a good horse died and a fine MFH-huntsman narrowly escaped being killed too. Hounds found in a covert close to the village and the fox went away unseen by Sidney, being holloaed beyond. I held open the gate for Ronnie as he galloped through and the field were soon far away except for a few stragglers."

It was later in the day when *"hounds settled down to run parallel with the Fosse, which they crossed near the Donnington turning. Ronnie came galloping out from* the side road on to the Fosse, with never a thought for anything but his hounds, who had gone over to mark their fox in some quarries a few fields further on.

A car coming from the direction of Stow hit Ronnie's horses broadside on, breaking a hind fetlock, whilst Ronnie himself fell on to the hard road on his back and must have been tremendously shaken by the impact. I didn't, fortunately, see the actual collision, but came upon Sidney holding his own horse and Ronnie's (who was Housewarmer, a former well-known 'chaser belonging to Dorothy Paget) and a woman on a bicycle seemed to be in attendance, having caught the poor old horse as he came down the road. Ronnie and all the Field were gathered at the cross-roads beyond.

Charles (Charles Parker, celebrated terrier-man to the Heythrop) was sent for and it was not long before he arrived and put the poor old horse out of his misery with the humane killer. He was eighteen years old and had been round the National course several times, finishing fourth in 1946. It was such a tragic and ignominious end. By the time I reached the cross-roads Ronnie was insisting upon going on hunting, obviously an impossibility, for he was very badly bruised and shaken. I was sorry, too,

Pond Cottage, Badminton, where Daphne lived for over 40 years, from 1958 until she moved to a nursing home in Tetbury.

for the men in the car who were, I believe, terribly upset."

"All persuasion having failed to make Ronnie go home, Raymond Barrow decided to send the FIELD home instead and hope that Ronnie would not then make the attempt to go on. But, after all, Bill Scott was appointed Deputy-Huntsman, and though some of the field had already departed, messages were sent North, South, East & West to bring them back and I don't think that many missed the subsequent hunt. Hounds had very fortunately run their fox to ground in the quarry across the main road, so were easily stopped. It was decided that Bill should draw the Pole Covert, near Upper Swell.

Quite a long hack on, and luckily I had a lift there, so arrived in time to climb that steep slope up to the wood and be there when hounds found their fox and went away. It

was just one o'clock when they first opened on the line and thereafter were hunting for 2¼ hours – a most creditable performance on the part of their huntsman. He has been helping to whip-in since Durno's accident after the Opening Meet, but that is rather different to being huntsman to a virtually strange pack of hounds, to say nothing of having a strange horn to blow!

The fox broke on the south side and I was soon left far behind, but after emerging on to the road I heard a voice offering me a lift and found it to be none other than RONNIE, who, instead of being in hospital, or at the very least in bed, was following round, with Peggy driving the car. So I got in and we drove to Upper Swell (hounds having previously made a circle above Nether Swell) and then on our right was the fox going in the direction of Donnington Brewery.

Hounds had just come to a check, so Ronnie told me to run and tell Bill, who was now at the top of an almost perpendicular bank. Fortunately Bob Brackenbury (the Warwickshire Master) took the message from me, so saved me a heart attack.

Hounds struck the line and I followed on foot, losing them temporarily in the bottom, but getting a lift on with a follower from Shipton-under-Wychwood who had already taken me earlier in the day to Pole Covert. Hounds had gone on to Banks Fee Farm and from there to Banks Fee. I just caught sight of their fox as he crossed the main road a yard or two in front of the leading hounds and ran right handed towards Duncombe House.

Turning south, they ran below Abbotswood and to the left of Pole Covert. It was quite reminiscent of the old North Cotswold days to hear Bill approaching his fences with a volley of curses, or galloping along swearing vociferously, sometimes at his horse and sometimes at nothing at all! Approaching Pole Covert, we only pulled up in the car just in time, for we didn't know hounds were running so close to us on our left, and in terror of Bill's wrath, we buried our heads on our knees and hoped we weren't recognised! I took to my feet again here and got left well behind, hounds running on to Eyford, but finally obtained another lift and caught up at a check at Swell Hill.

A hare jumped up in front of the pack and several people, myself included I'm ashamed to say, thought hounds were hunting her when they hit off the line again exactly in the direction in which she went.

But we maligned them. Their fox had taken a similar line, and they crossed the road, more slowly now. Scent eventually fading out not far from Condicote. I had run this latter part and felt proud that I had held open the first gate of the day for Ronnie and the last gate of the day for his successor! It was now three-fifteen; a very good hunt to end a rather disastrous day.

The memorial plaque for Charles Parker on a bridge over the river Blackwater in Ireland where his ashes were scattered. When he left the Heythrop, where he had been a legendary terrierman, organising all the earthstopping and otterhunting all summer, he became official 'harbourer' to the Devon and Somerset Staghounds on Exmoor, where his skills as a naturalist were again made full use of. He then moved to Ireland, where he organised the gardens for Captain and Mrs Evan Williams, a skill he had always practised, but was not so well known for.

I should have mentioned that Albert Buckle was out (now huntsman to the Whaddon Chase), and he assisted to whip-in. There were a great many visitors: Colonel John Scott of the Buccleuch among them; also Anthony Hart, Master of the Cotswold Vale, mounted by Ronnie. This evening I rang up to inquire for the poor invalid and was surprised when he answered the telephone. He was in bed, very sore and bruised, but the X-ray revealed no broken bones and he sounded quite cheerful."

A local newspaper report said: *"Major Scott has shown that he has lost none of his art and despite hunting strange hounds, he has shown excellent sport."*

He hunted hounds for the ensuing week, killed a brace of foxes one day, and produced a five-mile point on the next. *"Major Scott"*, went on the report, *"was of course still wearing his red coat. Have the Heythrop hounds ever been hunted by anyone wearing that colour before?"* It is almost certain that the answer would be in the negative.

In August 1958, recording the first morning's cubhunting with the Duke of Beaufort's bitch pack in her diary, Daphne starts by saying: *"I have scarcely missed a "first morning" from Badminton for the past 10 or 11 years, but little knew that I should, this season, be hunting from home at Pond Cottage, Badminton."*

Considering the enormity of the change in her life, this seems somewhat understated. It would seem that Master had invited her to come and live at Badminton on a "grace and favour" basis, but she was not able to leave her mother, in failing health, at Tewkesbury. Her mother died in February that year, which left Daphne, now forty-eight years old, free at last to leave The Gastons and take up Master's offer. Daphne was, of course, now in seventh heaven, living in the shadow of Badminton House. *"Living within earshot of the kennels one wakens to a dawn chorus of hound music; in winter's early morning there is always the cheerful clatter of horses' hoofs as the hunters set off for their exercise; often a foxhound puppy comes to meet one in the drive. Here, surely, Foxhunting has its true home."*

Perhaps the spirit of Badminton is best summed up by the 19th Lord Willoughby de Broke, who wrote: *"Foxhunting seems to be rooted in the soil. The stately home almost merges in the kennel. The first thing that meets you in the precincts is always a foxhound, walking about with a self-satisfied air of assured*

Captain Ian Farquhar, Master and huntsman of the Duke of Beaufort's Hounds since 1974, with hounds at Pond Farm, Shipton Moyne, followed by kennel-huntsman and first whipper-in, Tony Holdsworth, who took over the hunting of the hounds in 2010, and second whipper-in, Paul Hardwick.

proprietorship... At Badminton the stud and the pack are integral portions of the establishment. Like their Master, they did not come there yesterday and they will not be gone to-morrow. They have a traditional home within the very stones of Badminton; their predecessors have been there in some form or another ever since there was a Duke of Beaufort."

Despite Daphne's criticism of him as a huntsman, Gerald Gundry was a wonderful Joint Master. A grandson of the legendary "Parson" Milne of the Cattistock, he had hunted the Eton Beagles and the Goathland foxhounds before commanding his old regiment, the 16th/5th Lancers, during the war.

He knew every farmer in the Beaufort country personally – and the

Christian names of all their families – he was much in demand as a gifted and entertaining after-dinner speaker and always carried fence-mending tools in his vehicle.

However, Daphne continued, commenting on a September cubhunting day. *"Percival Williams, the Master of the Four Burrow in Cornwall, arrived to stay at Badminton for cubhunting today at Silk Wood. It was a poor morning – poor scent, poor huntsman! At one point Gerald completely lost all his hounds in Silk Wood and 19 couple of them joined themselves to Master! I think he has now become very deaf, which is of course a severe handicap."*

It would seem that Daphne's riding days were now over as she notes: *"John Miller (later Crown Equerry) has invited me to go up to Melton with him next Sunday and ride his Saddle Club horses with the Quorn (Monday), Cottesmore (Tuesday) and Belvoir (Wednesday). It sounded like Heaven and years ago I would have jumped at the chance, but now I doubt whether I have either the nerve or the clothes – both are a bit threadbare!"*

But Daphne continued to enjoy some wonderful hunting. With the Portman in December she writes: *"Today was splendid; a magnificent hound-hunt without a lot of scent, but with amazing perseverance on the part of Sir Peter and his foxhounds, literally walking their fox to death!"*

Writing a report later she describes the hunt in question: *"Hounds were hack-ing through the village of Monkton St Giles on their way to draw a kale field just beyond, when they suddenly threw up their heads, obviously winding a fox, and then crashed over the fence into some bushes behind the churchyard and were immediately away with their fox!*

They ran very fast to the Gussage St Giles road, up which the fox had run for half a mile. He then left it, immediately to run through a flock of hurdled sheep. These manoeuvres gave him a good start, and hounds could only hunt on slowly to the Pinetum, and then into St Giles Park, where a huge herd of heifers further complicated matters.

Realising that something had to be done to get them on terms with their fox again, the huntsman cast right on forrard over the Cranborne-Wimborne road, round Rye Hill and into the narrow part of the Roughs, when they hit off the line. Hounds then settled well, and hunted on into Kingswood.

Here a fresh fox sprang out of some thick brambles, almost into the middle of the pack: about half the hounds pursued him, and as it was impossible in this big wood to

Four famous retired foxhunters pictured at Peterborough Show in 1969.
Left to right: Stanley Barker, huntsman Pytchley; Percy Durno, huntsman Heythrop; Sir Peter Farquhar,
lastly Master and huntsman of the Portman; and George Gillson, huntsman, Warwickshire and
Meynell.

get to their heads to stop them, they raced screaming after him, while the rest went on slowly hunting their original fox.

After about 10 minutes there occurred what the huntsman considers was almost unique in his experience — the hounds hunting the fresh fox started leaving that one OF THEIR OWN ACCORD, and returned a few at a time to join the rest, and in a few minutes the entire pack was reunited on the line of their hunted fox! They came away from Kingswood at the southern end and ran across the open towards Horton, making a wide left-handed circle round Woodlands to enter Boys Wood.

The fox was now obviously tiring and was running the rides, and here another curious thing happened: a lady walking down a ride with two dogs on leads told the huntsman that she and the fox had met in the ride, that he had taken no notice of her, but had galloped on straight past her, nearly knocking over her dog as he passed!

Coming out onto the road at the far end of the wood, he gained a little breathing space for himself by running the road for some way, but hounds hit off the line again into Birches, and from their cry it was obvious their fox was now being hard pressed. They pushed him away from Birches, and with Pains Moor on their left screamed down to the brook, and turned right handed along it. Crossing the road by Verwood station, they swung right handed into Ninny Copse, where they caught him after a really remarkable hound hunt of 2 hours and 5 minutes with a point of four and a half miles."

Daphne completes her diary note: *"Peter was simply delighted with the way his hounds had worked, and no wonder!"*

The same week, the Duke of Beaufort's bitch pack produced a fine

hunt from their meet at the Kennels. *"Such a good day, with a real old-fashioned sort of hunt, hounds running, as Master said, just like they used to in the old days and not simply from one kale field to another."*

Finding in The Verge and going away by Castle Barn, hounds covered a great deal of both the Saturday and Monday country, completing the hunt through Hinnegar, running out to the far end of Swangrove and turning back to kill their fox after an exceptional hunt of 3 hours 10 minutes, with points of 7½ miles and 4½ miles and covering more than 22 miles as they ran.

Now happily installed at Badminton, Daphne's life seemed perfect. There was more and more writing to be done, with hunting reports, articles in the sporting press and coverage of the Hound Shows during the summer months.

Her first book was published in 1964 – *The Book of the Foxhound*, to be followed in 1974 by her hunting autobiography, *In Nimrod's Footsteps*. Then *Famous Foxhunters* in 1978 and *Foxhounds* in 1981. She was centrally based at Badminton to hunt with many of the great packs of hounds. Hunting had come back after the war stronger than ever and sport was of the highest order.

CHAPTER FOURTEEN

The Final Years

There were two particularly historic meets at Badminton that stand out in Daphne's memory in 1960 and 1970 respectively.

The first event, in 1960, was to commemorate the Duke's 60th birthday, when he hunted hounds himself, and the other meet was to mark the occasion of his 70th, after he had handed over the hunting of the hounds to professional huntsman,

Brian Gupwell, in 1967. On March 26th 1960 Daphne writes in her diary: *"Master celebrates his 60th birthday on April 4th and his birthday present from past and present Members of the Hunt was presented at today's Badminton 'lawn meet' – the first of its kind for many years."*

She continues in her article for *Horse & Hound*: *"It was on this very spot that Barraud painted his well-known picture of 1840, "Lawn Meet at Badminton," and* since then many a famous lawn meet has taken place here, immortalised in diaries and memoirs of days long past; but never has there been a more important occasion than that of last Saturday.

A field of some 200 assembled on their horses, whilst in front was a crowd nearly 500 strong. The Duke himself, Col Cox-Cox, the Hunt Chairman, and Major General Sir Stewart Menzies, the oldest wearer of the "Blue-and-Buff" hunting today, occupied a wagon drawn up in the drive outside the front door. A sum of £650 had been subscribed towards the birthday present, which took the form of a Minton breakfast service – a copy of one which had been used at Badminton for about 100 years; this cost approximately half the total sum, and the residue was to be given towards buying the best hunter that money could buy." [This is an interesting reminder of the value of both fine china and horseflesh in 1960!]

'Master' at a meet at Badminton in 1960, when he hunted his hounds on the occasion of his 60th birthday.

'Master' following his hounds, now hunted by professional, Brian Gupwell, following his 70th birthday meet at Badminton House.

"Sir Steward Menzies began hunting with the ducal pack in 1912, when the 9th Duke was Master and huntsman. His speech was full of reminiscences and was a remarkably good one, without recourse to notes of any kind. He recalled the days of the Duke's father, his extraordinary successful – and breath taking – long-distance casts, and remarked that, could he have been present on this occasion, it would undoubtedly have been the happiest day of his life to see his illustrious pupil, his successor, the 10th Duke. A total of 84 consecutive years between father and son as Masters and huntsmen must be a record seldom, if ever, equalled.

In a most interesting and at times amusing speech the Duke spoke of the "labour of love" which he had experienced by 40 years hunting his own hounds, and said that he found the thrill as great today, when hounds leave kennels for a day's hunting, as it was to him 40 years ago. Today was the 2885th day he had hunted hounds, and to him there was never a bad day's hunting; some were just not so good as others. Today, he said, sons and grandsons of the men who hunted with him in the 1920s were now members of the Hunt; the farmers still provided a welcome as did their fathers and grandfathers of old.

Good hounds and good foxes were necessary to sport, and in his opinion his hounds were now as good as he ever had, whilst the foxes this season had run better, straighter and faster than for many years past.

The future of foxhunting in this country was good, and he asked everyone to drink Success to Foxhunting. Hounds were then brought across from their kennels, a few hundred yards distant, and a gallant cavalcade moved off up the avenue of the ancient park, away from the scene of this historic meet, for a most enjoyable day's hunting."

Sir Rupert Buchanan-Jardine, who hunted the Dumfriesshire hounds for his father and successfully continued his breeding policies, maintaining their nose, colour and deep booming cry.

A few days' later was the Duke's actual birthday, when he hunted hounds from North Wraxall and Daphne's diary starts:

"2,288 is a very remarkable score:
On April 4th at 60 not out,
May you add to it many runs more!

I made up this bit of doggerel for a birthday card to go with Master's birthday present of a large silk hunting handkerchief. He has killed 2,288 foxes up to this morning's meet."

Ten years later a great day's sport followed the Duke's 70th birthday meet, which was held at Worcester Lodge at the north end of Badminton Park.

"An afternoon fox provided a flying hunt which ended (after a first class gallop for those still left out) at the very gates of the kennels, where hounds rolled over their tired fox at the very feet of the Duke himself – a fitting finish to an historic day."

At this time Allan Garrigan was kennel-boy and rode second horse for  Brian Gupwell. He lived with the other single lads working with the horses in the bothy above the stables and used to call in on Daphne once or twice a week for tea and cake. He was one of several young people who were keen on hounds that she encouraged and spent time with, continuing to write to him when he moved on in hunt service.

Most interestingly he witnessed the last day that Daphne went otterhunting. She had not followed the otterhounds regularly since the 1950s, which was mostly due to the fact that it was by attending the hound shows and puppy shows in the summer months that she earned most of her writing fees. She also, almost certainly, recognised that the otter as a species was becoming scarcer and, as a conservationist and naturalist, she would not have felt comfortable adding to its pressures. It was of course at this time that the otterhound packs were changing to hunting mink, which were increasingly becoming a serious pest on the rivers.

On the day in question in 1969, the Hawkstone met at the Berkeley Arms close by the Castle and kennels, and Daphne donned her blue and red Hawkstone uniform and drove her grey mini van to the meet. Having drawn blank for some time, hounds were taken to the ponds behind Leyhill Prison, where they immediately ran with a great cry, encouraged by their Master and huntsman Michael Downes. Jack Stallard, who had been

Captain Evan Williams with his wife Jill, Sir Peter Farquhar and Daphne Moore, pictured at Peterborough Show in 1966, the year his hound, Tipperary Grizzle '64, was Bitch Champion.

their kennel-huntsman since the war, was not impressed. *"They like the smell of the lilies,"* he said: *"Last week it was Muscovy ducks."* Daphne was even less impressed and announced that it was her last day's otterhunting – and it was.

Back in 1958 Daphne was busier than ever on the Puppy Show and Hound Show circuit for Horse & Hound and this year included the premier Irish Hound Show held at Clonmel.

"I stayed for Clonmel with Mrs Hall, the evergreen 'Miss'us' of the Carlow, whose beautiful Patchwork '57 won the Bitch Championship; this was a Carlow victory for the third successive year. The Tipperary were the runners-up with Charity '57; This must have brought great satisfaction to dear old Ikey Bell, who was watching from the ringside, since he had been Fairy Godfather to the "Tipps" ever since the accession to the Mastership of Evan Williams in 1953."

Evan Williams had preceded his hunting life with a distinguished career as a professional jockey. He won the 1937 Grand National on Royal Mail and the 1936 Cheltenham Gold Cup on Golden Miller and in 1940 on Roman Hackle. In 1966 Evan Williams won the Bitch Championship at Peterborough with Tipperary Grizzle '64, the first Irish Champion since 1928 when Carlow Vera '23 had won. Daphne noted in her show catalogue: *"How I wish Ikey were alive to witness this triumph, since the Tipps were so largely built up by him at the start of Evan's Mastership."*

As she got older Daphne did not travel too far afield to follow other packs of hounds, but she did not miss many days with the Beaufort. She still attended all the hound shows, though, and many puppy shows, all of which she wrote up for *Horse and Hound*. She was often driven by her good friend, Miss "Tuppy" Pearson. Master relied on her to keep up his pedigree books and to make his entries in the *Foxhound Kennel Stud Book* and for the hound shows.

It was the latter duty that caused a celebrated incident at Peterborough Show in 1981. The serious problem arose when it was noticed on the morning of the show that the Duke of Beaufort's hounds had not been entered in the class for unentered bitches, the second class in the afternoon. It seemed that Daphne may have suffered a lapse of concentration when making the entries and confused the first unentered class, for which the Beaufort were ineligible, being restricted to packs that had not won prizes at Peterborough in recent years, with the second, open class for unentered bitches, failing to ensure that the Beaufort were entered in the latter. Master had already won the unentered doghounds class in the morning and no doubt expected his young bitches to do as well.

Master demanded that the omitted entry should be overlooked and his hounds included in the class which he intended them to be in.

A hasty meeting of the Peterborough committee was held and Lt. Colonel Tony Murray Smith, former Master of the Fernie and the Quorn, was given the unenviable task of braving the wrath of a very disappointed Duke by telling him that the rules had to stand and no exceptions could be made.

Master, who took his showing very seriously, was very angry indeed and said so in no uncertain terms, but his hounds were not shown in the class.

The ducal fury, always short-lived, gave way to benign smiles when he won the Bitch Championship. However, to poor Daphne this was a complete disaster and, totally mortified, she retreated weeping to the car park to regain her composure.

Legend has it that Daphne was so upset that she did not wait for the Duke's car to drive her back to Badminton, but went home alone on the train from Peterborough. As usual, the Duke's ire was of a very brief duration and Daphne remained a valued friend to both him and the Duchess.

Daphne took great trouble to encourage the young who showed an interest in hunting. Lord Mancroft, now Chairman of the Masters of Foxhounds Association, re-members that, as a child living in Badminton village, he always referred to Daphne as "the walker". This would have been due to her, being a lady of a certain age, still following hounds on foot whenever possible and going about her business in the village at a brisk walk or jog. She also wrote to him as a boy at prep school to tell him about the sport being shown by the Beaufort hounds and any other local topics of interest.

Kay Gardner, now an author in her own right, remembers first meeting Daphne as a 12-year-old. Kay's father took the *Shooting Times*, in which Daphne wrote regular articles about hunting, and Kay became an avid reader of these.

As she grew up, not being able to afford to hunt on a horse, Kay followed by bicycle and regularly met Daphne, who, perhaps recognising the young lady as being in a similar position to herself at that age, took Kay under her wing.

If they were following by car, Daphne and "Tuppy" Pearson would often take Kay with them and afterwards, she remembers, there would be tea at Pond Cottage with "lashings of honey" when every hunt would be discussed in minute detail.

She recalls that *"despite over 50 years disparity in age, we soon struck up a lively correspondence of letters and telephone calls. With our shared love of hounds and our native Gloucestershire, we were never short of things to talk about."*

Kay also remember how Daphne encouraged her own writing career, giving her constructive advice, even though she was writing about similar subjects and reporting on puppy shows.

Another young person who was befriended by Daphne was Edward Knowles, who was working at the Estate Office at Badminton. He had previously hunted the Royal Agricultural College Beagles and was whipping-in as an amateur to Ian Farquhar at the Beaufort. He later went on to be Joint Master and huntsman of the South Dorset and is presently at the Tedworth.

Daphne left Edward her full set of *Foxhound Kennel Stud Books* – surely the most thumbed of any in the land – and containing many of her own notes and other letters. Interestingly, Edward remembers her talking about Harry Glynn and telling him that Harry was the man that she would have married, had he not been killed in the war.

In 1974 Michael Clayton became editor of *Horse and Hound*. He had previously been an international television and radio reporter for the BBC, including war reporting in Vietnam, Cambodia and the Middle East. Before that he had worked as a Fleet Street journalist with the *London Evening News* and the *Evening Standard*.

Horse and Hound magazine were extraordinarily lucky to have a man

'Master', 10th Duke of Beaufort, pictured at his 70th birthday meet.

of his experience at the helm. But Michael was a passionate foxhunter, having been brought up as a member of the Portman Pony Club in Dorset and, when working in London, hunting whenever he could with the Old Surrey and Burstow.

At *Horse & Hound* he took on the role of hunting correspondent himself, writing weekly articles on his hunting visits under the title of "Foxford's Hunting Diary" – Foxford being one

The American, 'Ikey' Bell in old age, living in Ireland. He probably had more influence on the development of the modern foxhound than anyone else and was a good friend of Daphne's, regularly corresponding with her.

of his favourite hunters – and basing his regular hunting in the Portman, the Whaddon Chase and, finally, in High Leicestershire.

He remembers: *"When I gave up foreign news reporting, including the war zones, I thought my most exciting adventures were over. Riding strange horses in new hunting countries afforded me more thrills than I could have imagined, and in a setting I grew to love deeply."*

Michael Clayton inherited regular correspondents for each area of the horse world. One who often covered hunting matters was none other than Daphne's good friend "Bay" de Courcy-Parry who wrote as "Dalesman", and Daphne herself of course had written about all matters concerning hounds for many years.

Daphne's relationship with the new Editor was at times tricky. She did not appreciate the discipline he

Michael Clayton, a highly respected national journalist and broadcaster, who was Editor of Horse and Hound for 24 years and employed Daphne throughout that time. A passionate foxhunter, he has written the Preface to this book.

necessarily exerted over timing, length and content of articles. He, however, valued her skills saying: *"She always wrote well, never really criticising anything in 'modern' hound breeding, but reviled 'Old English' hounds, which she imbibed from Ikey Bell and Master. This is made very clear in her excellent Book of the Foxhound. Most of her actual hunting experience with foxhounds was in the West and South Midlands, but she was fortunate to see some very good huntsmen and packs of hounds at work. She had a very clear idea of what good standards amounted to in foxhunting, and her views on breeding were sound, except her imbalance on the subject of 'Old English'."*

Michael Clayton continues: *"She was a remarkable woman, with great strength of will. Dealing with her on the phone when she launched into one of her interminable "queries on my expenses" was a mind-numbing task for my staff. Sometimes I would have to intervene, and I usually gave in to her demands.*

We only had one upset, when Master complained that we had cut her report of his Puppy Show, and we were able to show that we had not. Clearly this had been her response to him when he complained about its quality and length in "doing justice" to his hounds.

Considering that Daphne depended very heavily on every penny she earned in journalistic fees and expenses, and desperately depended on Master for her home and livelihood, all this is understandable, and I personally admired her courage and her determination to preserve her way of life until a great age – which she managed to achieve.

Clearly Daphne's hectic physical life in the hunting field, including a great deal of following hounds on foot, gave her an exceptionally strong constitution. She remained mentally alert until the end, and continued to write until a great age."

Naturally, the death of the Duke of Beaufort in February 1984 and that of the Duchess three years later was a shattering blow for Daphne. She had been devoted to Master and Mary – and their numerous dogs – since her first visit to Badminton and had enjoyed their kindness and friendship ever since. As they were without children, the title and estate were passed to Master's cousin, David Somerset, who had already been a Joint Master for a decade and, being an exceptional horseman (he was second at Badminton Horse Trials), had acted as Field Master throughout that time.

He continued to look after Daphne in every way he could and she was included in all hunting activities on the estate and within the Hunt. With many business interests in London, the new Duke needed someone to run the hunting for him and in 1985 he persuaded Captain Ian Farquhar to move from the Bicester country, where he had enjoyed thirteen very successful seasons as Master and huntsman, to Badminton to fulfil the same duties. Ian had great connections

In her later diaries, there are fewer and fewer of Daphne's small watercolours in the margins with which she had illustrated specific incidents which had occurred during a day's hunting, as above.

198

with Badminton as his father, Sir Peter Farquhar, a lifelong friend of Master's, had moved close by when he gave up the Portman country in 1959.

Daphne of course was delighted that a son of Sir Peter's should take over at Badminton, especially as, like his father, he favoured new Welsh outcrosses. He hunted hounds more in the style of the old Duke, rather than in the rather noisier, hands-on style of a professional huntsman such as Brian Gupwell, who had been hunting the Duke of Beaufort's hounds since Master handed over the horn in 1967.

By now Daphne was 75 years old and undoubtedly getting more eccentric. Her latter years at Pond Cottage were hampered by what we now call OCD and she became somewhat reclusive with all but her very closest friends. Both Ian Farquhar and Lord Mancroft talk of the somewhat overpowering smell of carbolic soap and Dettol at Pond Cottage and of her answering the door in rubber gloves. But she kept attending the shows, driven by her loyal friend Tuppy Pearson.

For many years she wore the same grey suit at the Badminton Puppy Show and carried a clipboard to all the shows, with a plastic cover in case of rain – even on the sunniest day. Her

Daphne Moore attending her last puppy show at Badminton in her 90s, but still with clipboard at the ready to write the day up for Horse and Hound.

increasing paranoia extended even to the staff in the house. I myself remember her leaning towards me at a lunch at Badminton House before the Puppy Show and saying *"I won't get any food you know. This butler doesn't like me – just you wait and see!"*

However, her sense of humour

The family grave of the Moore family under the walls of Tewkesbury Abbey. Daphne was the last to be added in 2004.

predeceased her by a year, talking weekly on the telephone. John's death at the tragically early age of 59 had been a terrible shock to Daphne, although their relationship had not always been an easy one. It has been suggested that he disapproved of hunting which may have been the cause, but much of his work shows a deep understanding of its romance, which included otterhunting:

"As I walked, the hounds passed me, padding along so circumspectly with waving sterns and lifted head that I could have shouted for the love of them... for their music made me mad and drunk with the sound of it and they can lead me to the river as the Pied Piper led the rats at Hamelin... Dexter, Bellman, Pitiful, Dancer, Dairymaid: I hear them in dreams, great voices belling deep down in a stream along the rocks, solitary tongues calling, threatening, yelling for blood; and then the crash of the whole pack in unison, which is like no other sound in the whole world. Next time I hear it I shall be after them as hard as I can go."

never failed her. In 1991 she wrote to Kay Gardner after failing to win a British Field Sports Society raffle:

"Of course I am devastated not to have won the holiday in Barbados. I already had at least a dozen partners lined up, and have bought a very dashing bikini..."

She maintained contact with her brother's widow Lucile, who

Indeed, as David Cole, John Moore's biographer, says... *"he did tire of hunting and left his sister to continue that particular family tradition. He would always* remain, however, a vocal advocate for the practicalities of the sport. *"I am no dyed in the wool foxhunter – in fact I am squeamish about the kill and the dig – but foxes must be killed – even the antis agree to that – surely it is a question of alternatives; If I were a fox I think I should prefer a two-to-one chance of escape or the immediacy of a snap of the jaws to the slow festering of the gunshot wound, or the bitter gripe of poison. Or the long dark agony of the trap, waiting, waiting for the dreaded trapper to come in the morning."*

David Cole continues:

"Moore thought his urban readership largely misunderstood the purpose of hunting with hounds and continually returned to the subject during his time with the Birmingham Mail. Steeped in family hunting tradition – with a sister who devoted her whole life to the sport – he always remained a supporter of the practicalities and ethics of the chase."

Eventually ill health and infirmity made it necessary for David Beaufort to arrange for Daphne to move to the Priory Nursing Home in Tetbury.

Although it was hard for her to accept, she had many regular visitors including Anthony Hart, by then Secretary of the Master of Foxhounds Association, to whom she left her treasured hunting diaries.

Harry Parsons, who is renowned for his pack of Sealyham terriers, says he was always fascinated by her articles and visited her several times in the last year of her life. He says that, sadly, her short term memory had gone – she thought that her brother John was still alive – but that she remembered the old days very clearly. She talked of otterhunting with Arthur Jones and Pip Stanier and could remember hounds' names and pedigrees.

She also talked of Harry Glynn, with whom he says she had definitely been in love. Kay Gardner, her most regular visitor, says that *"years of outdoor living meant that she always had the windows of her room wide open, which drove her carers mad! She had asked for bird feeders and nesting boxes to be placed outside her windows and her feathered friends were often in the room with her and provided a constant source of amusement. I was permitted to take my terrier, and she would always say 'oh do let the little darling up on the bed…' She still loved to see her old friends and the odd canine visitor."*

On July 6th 2004, Daphne Moore died at the Priory Nursing Home in Tetbury. There was a small gathering for her simple funeral at West Leigh crematorium and the Eulogy was given by Mike Pinker, an old friend who ran the Ladyswood Shooting School in the Sodbury Vale. Kay Gardner read the iconic Will Ogilvie poem:

The dusk is down on the river meadows,
The moon is climbing above the fir,
The lane is crowded with evening shadows,
The gorse is only a distant blur.
The last of the light is almost gone,
But hark! They're running!
They're running on!
The count of the years is steadily growing;
The Old give way to the eager Young;
Far on the hill is the horn still blowing,
Far on the steep are the hounds still strung.
Good men follow the good men gone;
And hark! They're running!
They're running on!

On 31st July 2004, a half-page obituary appeared in *The Times* – a recognition of an extraordinary life, which would undoubtedly have surprised Daphne herself.

As was the case with her brother John, there was no memorial service and her ashes were interred, without ceremony, in the family plot beneath the walls of Tewkesbury Abbey, where a stone is inscribed:

In loving memory of
CECIL CHARLES MOORE
Died February 15th 1918
Aged 56
And of his wife
ELIZA GEORGINA
Died February 16th 1958
Aged 84

And of their son
JOHN MOORE
Born November 10th 1907
Died July 27th 1967
Aged 59
And loving wife
LUCILE née STEPHENS
Born June 4th 1916
Died September 6th 2003
Aged 87

And of his sister
DAPHNE MARY MOORE
Born May 3rd 1910
Died July 6th 2004
Aged 94

Daphne had lived a life that was frugal, eccentric, and perhaps obsessive. Despite the early family misfortunes and the personal devastation that the war caused her, she remained steadfast in her deep passion for hounds and hunting, which she communicated with such skill through her writing and these diaries.

Badminton seemed the appropriate place for a plaque to be installed in memory of Daphne Moore. Pictured here in the Beaufort kennels (left to right): Nick Hopkins (kennel huntsman to Duke of Beaufort's Foxhounds), Captain Ian Farquhar (Joint Master, Duke of Beaufort's Foxhounds), Simon Hart MP (Chairman of Countryside Alliance), Alastair Jackson (author), Michael O'Reilly (owner of the diaries) and Matt Ramsden (Joint Master and Huntsman, Duke of Beaufort's Foxhounds). The foxhounds are (l to r): Folkstone'14 and Fontwell'14; the pure-breed otterhounds are Daisy and Bluebell. This photo was taken 19 March 2018.

The Badminton Daphne Moore memorial plaque commissioned by Michael O'Reilly.

A young Ronnie Wallace leading out the Eton Beagles

Index

Also published by Merlin Unwin Books
_____

A Short History of Foxhunting Alastair Jackson & Michael Clayton

The Ride of my Life Michael Clayton

Right Royal John Masefield

The Byerley Turk Jeremy James

Saddletramp Jeremy James

Vagabond Jeremy James

The Tack Room Paula Sells

Horse Racing Terms Rosemary Coates

Horse Games Bob Thompson

The Racingman's Bedside Book Julian Bedford

www.merlinunwin.co.uk